Wyatt Earp
THE FILM AND THE FILMMAKERS

*"For my handling of the situation at Tombstone,
I have no regrets. Were it to be done over again,
I would do exactly as I did at that time. If the
outlaws and their friends and allies imagined
that they could intimidate or exterminate the
Earps by process of assassination, and then hide
behind alibis and the technicalities of the law,
they simply missed their guess."*

—WYATT EARP

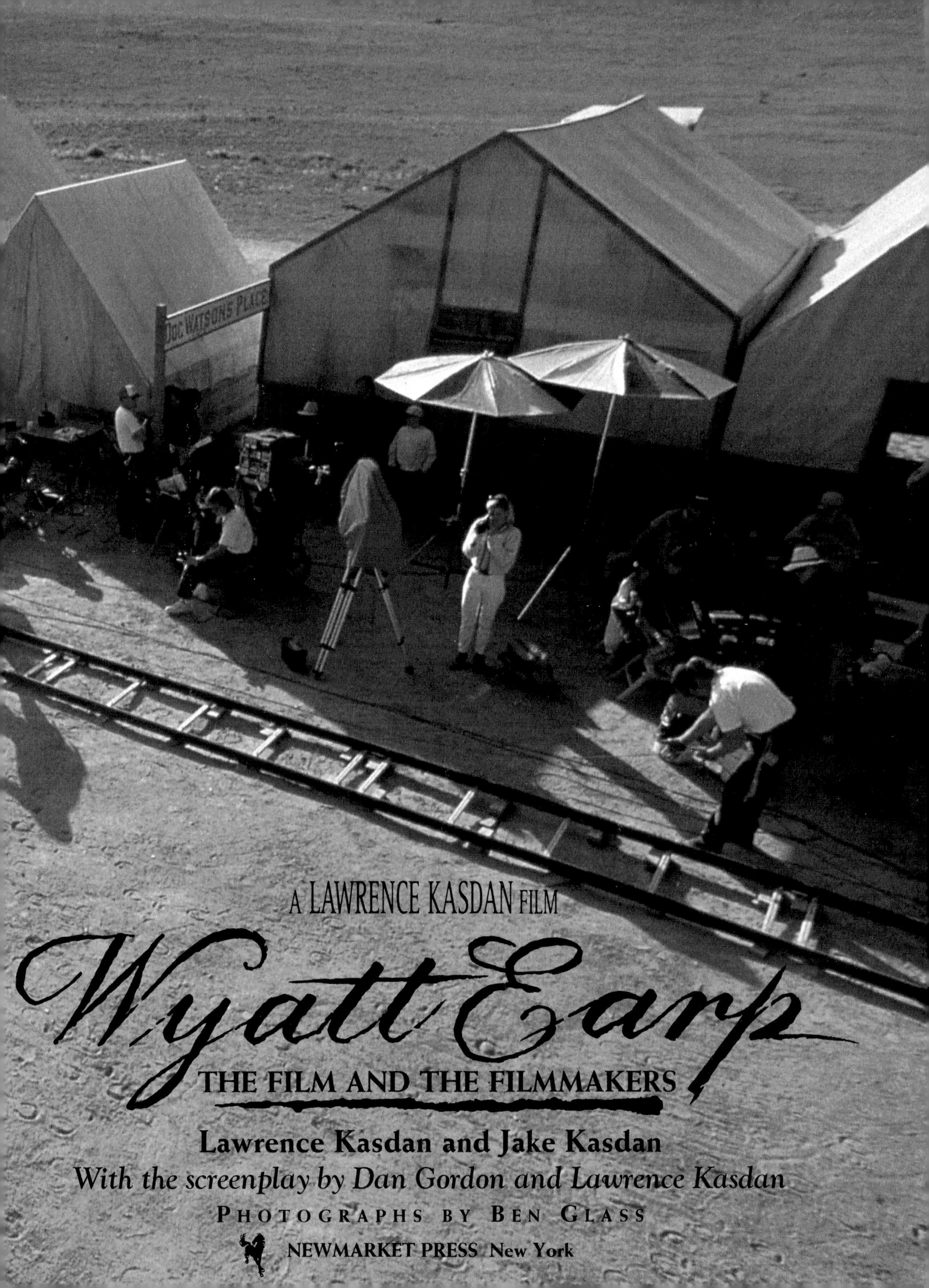

A LAWRENCE KASDAN FILM

Wyatt Earp

THE FILM AND THE FILMMAKERS

Lawrence Kasdan and Jake Kasdan

With the screenplay by Dan Gordon and Lawrence Kasdan

PHOTOGRAPHS BY BEN GLASS

NEWMARKET PRESS New York

94   95   96   97   10   9   8   7   6   5   4   3   2   1

Library of Congress Cataloging-in-Publication Data

Kasdan, Lawrence
    Wyatt Earp: the film and the filmmakers/Lawrence Kasdan and Jake Kasdan;
    introduction by Lawrence Kasdan; photographs by Ben Glass—1st ed.
    p.   cm. (A Newmarket pictorial moviebook)
    Includes bibliographical references.
    ISBN 1-55704-198-9
    1. Wyatt Earp (Motion picture) I. Kasdan, Jake. II. Title. III. Series.
PN1997.W93   1994
791.43'72—dc20   94-6296
                                                    CIP

Produced by Newmarket Productions, a division of Newmarket Publishing
& Communications Company: Esther Margolis, director, Keith Hollaman, editor,
Joe Gannon, production manager, Grace Farrell, assistant editor.

Book design by Deborah Daly

MANUFACTURED IN THE UNITED STATES OF AMERICA

First Edition

Other Newmarket Pictorial Moviebooks include:

CONTENTS

INTRODUCTION

"A man who can't be depended on steady isn't worth the trouble of havin' around."

BY DIRECTOR, PRODUCER AND CO-WRITER LAWRENCE KASDAN

The following has been extracted from Jake Kasdan's interviews with Lawrence Kasdan.

Wyatt's a certain kind of prototypical American hero with a lot of flaws. This movie attempts a depiction of the ages of man, from innocence to some sort of knowledge, with all the experience and cost that is required to obtain knowledge. You have to earn knowledge. Wyatt starts out as a blank slate who says he hopes he never has to kill anybody, but in the world that he inhabits he must become tougher and tougher. And it happens that he has a real proficiency for it. He has a knack for it. He thinks he wants to be a successful businessman, but the thing that he's really good at is being a lawman, which is not a way to get rich. It's like anyone in life who has certain ambitions but whose skills and talents are in another area. The Earps were great lawmen. That's the life they fell into, even though they tried to leave it.

"The first section of the movie is about his innocence and the tragedies that befall him. Wyatt starts to lose his optimistic view of life. The middle section of the movie is about finding his skills, becoming a lawman, and the people he becomes involved with during that transition. And in the last section of the movie, he

is formed. He's the man that he's going to be. Some of his ideas are good, some of them aren't flexible enough or nuanced enough to deal with a world that's complicated. He has become somebody who can't really change. He's become the man who must have the gunfight at the OK Corral.

"The facts of Wyatt's life make a very good story, a story about a man who walked down the center of this era, this very brief period that was the opening of the West. He was involved in many things. He helped supply the people who were building the transcontinental railroads. He hunted buffalo during the decimation of the great herds. He was a lawman in the cattle towns which were the source of all the wealth and economic vigor on the plains. And he continued to work in and travel through the West until the end of that era.

"I wanted to do a movie about Wyatt Earp because he epitomizes a very American journey. America started out with optimistic, innocent ideas. But in the settlement of America there was always a high level of violence and brutality. Americans have been good at it. We've

Kasdan (right)
with Director of
Photography
Owen Roizman

bravery, and it's stirring to see it, stirring to see people face up to their responsibilities in these situations, making tough choices. But you should not think that the movie says all these choices are right and that they are going to work out well, because this is a very sad story. And at the end, by the last scene, I hope that we can reach some sort of peace about it, a respite from the turmoil of these lives. But what has happened is tragic.

"Most of this script follows the history of these people very closely, but when you have this many characters there's some simplifying that goes on. Hopefully, what has emerged is a truth that's greater than the detail, a truth bigger than the facts. As they say in *The Man Who Shot Liberty Valance,* 'When the legend becomes fact, print the legend.' That's what we're doing, printing the legend. We've tried to find some truth that created this legend. We tried to find it, moment to moment, shot by shot. I hope that we can make people feel that they've been somewhere they've never been, that they've been there in a way that's real. That they really experienced it, that people talk like they might have talked if you'd been in the room with them. That's the goal. That's what I'm after. It's a hard thing to achieve because it's the truth, but it's the only thing I've known to go after since I started doing this. You don't always succeed, but you try every day. And we're always trying to raise our percentage of moments that are true.

"Westerns have always been very powerful for me. When I was growing up in West Virginia, I was seeing only American movies and many of those were Westerns, movies like *Gunfight at the OK Corral* and *The Magnificent Seven.* Then as I got older, I saw some of the Westerns from the thirties and forties, and some of those were very powerful to me. When I went to college I started seeing all of John Ford, Howard Hawks. *Red River* is a very important Western to me, also *My Darling Clementine, The Searchers, She Wore a Yellow Ribbon.* The Westerns of Anthony Mann, very neurotic, compulsive Westerns: *Bend of the River, The Man from Laramie, The Naked Spur.* What you saw when you saw the work of different directors and writers was that the Western genre was so large and so fluid and flexible that it could hold almost any kind of story.

been tough enough to face the challenges, but at some cost.

"This is really a story about a family. A family with a very strong patriarch with certain ideas about how life should be lived, what's important. This patriarch and his wife, who's also very strong, impart certain beliefs to their children so strongly, at a time when they are very impressionable, that the ramifications of those beliefs roll down over the years and influence everything that happens in their lives.

"I don't judge those ideas, but I know that nothing is as simple as some of those ideas. And what happened to the Earps, by following those ideas along for thirty years, was tragic. This is an American tragedy. There is real heroism here,

"And many of the stories that could be told there appealed to me. They were about heroism. They were about expansion. They were about people defining their lives in an environment in which there was very little definition, little law. Where people were making up their lives as they went along. People were struggling to make some sort of society. And the issue of how to conduct yourself when there are no rules is what I think all the work that I have done is about, on some level. Whether Western or not, that's what *Body Heat* is about, *The Big Chill*, *Grand Canyon*. The difficulty of leading an honorable life, given this tension that always exists between our ideals and our desires.

"Wyatt is very strongly inculcated with certain ideals. He is also very much a man. He wants things. He falls in love. He loses things. He suffers pain. He knows what his responsibilities are but he has desires which are sometimes in conflict with those responsibilities. All these things are very much in line with my interests. The Western is so large that you can do almost anything you want with it."

*Lawrence Kasdan,
below with Costner*

"EXCUSE ME, SIR. ARE YOU BY ANY CHANCE WYATT EARP?"

KEVIN COSTNER ON THE INITIAL
APPEAL OF WYATT EARP

From an actor's point of view, I'm very comfortable with the idea of being on a horse, with having guns on my sides, with the kind of ethic that must have ruled out there. It's in my psyche. I'm comfortable with that idea. From a producer's standpoint, for better or worse, my life is about making stories. Finding an original story is hard, and when you find one, you make it. Also, when you find a story that's familiar to you, you want to find an original way to make it—in a sense, to tell it the way you feel the story should be told. Wyatt Earp's is a story that I know and I wanted to share. There was a life that went well beyond the OK Corral. That always

intrigues me, because we have a tendency to see people in the media and attach a seminal moment to their life, but there's a whole set of events that led up to that moment and there's a whole life after that. I thought that a guy who could actually walk down the street to the OK Corral had to have had an interesting life. It's dangerous for a guy, with or without a badge, to walk into a saloon where people are drinking alcohol and wearing guns, and tell them to put their guns down. It's an unusual personality.

"Wyatt had tremendous resolve, and that got him into trouble because it was very difficult for him to look the other way. It was very clear who Wyatt Earp was. Everyone around him had to deal with

him on his own terms. He could be thought of as stiff or hard, but everyone was very clear about who it was they were dealing with. We know personalities like that and they can be hard to be around because they just don't cut anybody any slack. But they're also the kinds of personalities that attract intense loyalty.

"The fact is that thousands of people went through Tombstone, and this is the guy that people point to. He might be a myth in 1990, but in 1880 he was a fact. He was a fact that had to be dealt with. If you were in Tombstone and you wanted to do something, you either lined up with him or you lined up against him. That wasn't a myth or a legend, it was a fact of life. He was a very imposing character."

Costner with Producer Jim Wilson.

make, and each filmmaker does it differently. But when I feel as if I've read what I call the 'emotional truth,' then I'm very content to follow the facts of the script. [Also, I believe] you have to read between the lines of history. I know that the press very rarely gets anything right about me, even the simplest facts. When people try to identify this man by pointing at newspaper articles that were written in 1881, I think they're missing the point. You have to delve into the politics of the time. It's impossible for us to judge what was happening in 1881; we weren't there. I certainly wouldn't want my life explained by newspaper accounts, and have that held as fact."

AUTHENTICITY AND TRUTHFULNESS

Authenticity is important to me in every movie I do. I think when you enter into a world, you owe it to yourself to try to portray that world as realistically as possible. So if you enter into the world of people who were expanding the country just before the turn of the century, you need to try to portray the life. When people die, it should hurt. There should be something at stake. To me, realism is when one moment logically and realistically progresses to the next. Obviously, there are theatrical jumps that one has to

is torn between masculine ideas about how to act—what's the strong, right thing to do at all times—and the sensitive side which is torn by his conflicting desires. Kevin's very much a man of his heart, and you see that tension in Wyatt throughout the story. We're telling an epic story that spans thirty years. You see a man on the rack between what he feels he should do and what he wants to do. And that creates a good deal of tension.

"Kevin is very good at embodying that kind of tension between the urge to do right and the urge to fulfill his desires. Kevin also has a kind of grace which reminds me very much of not just Gary Cooper, whom he's often compared to, but Henry Fonda, who played Wyatt Earp in *My Darling Clementine*, in a performance that is almost dance-like— full of grace. Kevin has that kind of grace. Fonda moves in his own space. When you watch *My Darling Clementine* you see that. It's a wonderful film, a very odd film, very lyrical and poetic, almost elegiac. And Henry Fonda, in embodying Wyatt, always seems to be just a step slower than everyone else. He moves at his own pace with enormous authority. Kevin has that same kind of authority and has that unique physical presence."

LAWRENCE KASDAN ON COSTNER

A strong reason for me to do this was that I thought Kevin was born to play Wyatt. And Kevin, as an actor and as a star, embodies a lot of the straightforward American virtues that we most admire. You know, there's a kind of decency to Kevin and at the same time a muscular vigor to him. He's a masculine star and yet a very sensitive man. He's perfect to embody a large character who

"Blood counts the most."

The following is the original, unedited shooting screenplay.

INT. ORIENTAL SALOON, TOMBSTONE, ARIZONA (1881)—DAY
The place is almost deserted. A lone Bartender moves about behind the bar. There is only one patron, sitting at a table across the room, his back to us. Beyond him, the main source of light in the gloomy space is the swinging entrance door. The light catches in the smoke the man is exhaling.

CUT IN CLOSE on the surface of that table: a cup of coffee, some matches, a hat. A Colt .45 single-action revolver. A long-fingered hand holding a slim, burning cigar. Then, the back of his head, longish hair, neatly combed.

Two men come into the saloon and approach the man. Silhouettes against the light, we can't see them clearly.

> MORGAN
> They just moved out of the O.K. Corral, down by Fly's.

The sitting man nods.

> VIRGIL
> Looks like Ike, Billy, the McLaurys, and Billy Claiborne. Maybe more.

We still do not see the man's face. He takes the gun from the table, puts on his hat, and gets up.

> WYATT
> Let's go.

The three men go out the swinging door into the blinding sunlight. The door swings back and forth. WE STAY PUT.

LONG SLOW DISSOLVE TO:
EXT. CORNFIELD, PELLA, IOWA (1863)—DAY
The tall stalks wave in the wind. Blue sky and white clouds. A figure flashes down a row, running.

We're with him now— a farm boy, rangy, long-legged, starting to get muscles, raw-boned and handsome, fast on his feet. WYATT EARP at 15.

He stops abruptly, scoots through some stalks, kneels at a pile of cobs and digs out what he's hidden there. He stands in a hurry and disappears.

A CLEARING. Two boys are working the field, MORGAN (12) and WARREN (8). Wyatt bursts out of the corn. Over his shoulder is slung a pack and a thin bedroll. He runs up to the boys and puts his hand on Morgan's shoulder, then leans in and whispers something in his ear. Morgan smiles bravely and nods. Warren looks on, confused. Wyatt turns, speaks to him, then suddenly enfolds him in a hug that surprises them both. Just as quickly, Wyatt releases him and disappears back into the corn.

EXT. COUNTRY ROAD—DAY
Tall corn bounds the narrow dirt road as far as the eye can see. In the distance, the tiny figure of Wyatt, coming toward us, still running.

He reaches a bend in the road and suddenly skids to a halt, looking ahead. He darts quickly off the road.

EXT. CORNFIELD—DAY
Wyatt runs into the corn a short distance, then quietly turns and squats, trying to control the loud rasp of his breath.

HIS POV*: Through the leafy stalks, a Horseman can be intermittently seen cantering down the road. As he reaches the bend, he pulls up. The horse SNORTS, then the quiet returns. The SOUND of the wind and the rustling plants. Suddenly the Horseman turns into a row of corn and heads toward Wyatt.

Wyatt takes off at a run.

The Horseman steers his big mare skillfully through the maize, picking up speed.

Wyatt catches his foot on a root and goes head over heels. He is up instantly with startling grace and running again, but then jerks to a stop, disoriented. A GUST OF WIND shakes the surrounding stalks into noisy shudders. Wyatt peers around, looking for the Horseman. He plunges off through the thick corn.

Wyatt shoulders his way between two tight stalks, looking back at his pack, which has gotten hung up. He pulls it free with a mighty tug and spins— right into the head of the big, frothing mare. Wyatt trips backward, startled.

The Horseman is a big man of striking looks and bearing—NICHOLAS EARP.

*Point of View

2

NICHOLAS
Where you headed, Wyatt?

WYATT
Nowheres.

His father just looks down at him.

WYATT
I thought you went to Logan.

NICHOLAS
Changed my mind. Where you goin', son?

WYATT
To town.
          (quietly defiant)
I'm goin' to enlist, Pa. I want to fight the Rebs with James and Virg. I'm ready.

NICHOLAS
Are you?
          (Wyatt nods, hopeful)
Do you think your ma is ready?
          (Wyatt looks away)
I don't think she is.
          (he considers his son with some secret pride)
Where are the boys?

WYATT
In the cornfield. They can work it without me. They'll do just fine. I want to fight.

NICHOLAS
Why'd you wait till I left to take off, Wyatt? If you think it's the right thing?

Wyatt has been avoiding his gaze, but now, curiously, he looks his father in the eye. He's caught, but he won't make it worse with an excuse.

EXT. COUNTRY ROAD—DAY
Wyatt rides behind his father on the big mare.

NICHOLAS
Virgil and James should be coming on home someday soon now. Till they do, you know your job.

Wyatt nods, sullen.

NICHOLAS
What was that? I didn't hear you?

"REMEMBER THIS, ALL OF YOU..."

Nicholas Earp was a man in search of some kind of a dream. He was a man who moved around a lot. Started out in Missouri, then was married in Kentucky, then moved to Illinois, then to Iowa, and then to California. He had a family of seven children. He was a very strong character who managed in a time when it was very difficult to live in the Midwest and in the West. He managed to bring up a family, and have a career as an attorney, at the same time. He was successful in his latter life, too. He became a judge.

"He was a great believer in family. He felt that blood was the continuum of one's life, that everyone else was a stranger and that your only salvation in life was to stick with your brothers, your sisters, your mother, your father and your wife. And he passed that on to his children.

"He gave Wyatt guidance as to what it means to be a man, that you're a man of your work and that if you start a job, you finish it. Integrity was everything to Nicholas Earp, and I think he instilled that part of himself in Wyatt.

"He prepares his kids in a way that most fathers in those days had to prepare their children to live in those times, which were very tough. It was a very hard life. One had to be prepared to live off the land without amenities. This

made for very hard people with very difficult values. At least, we might find that survivalist mentality difficult in this day and age. But they were interesting characters.

"I think Nicholas was probably a very strong patriarch, but at the same time I think that all the moving was probably very distressful for the family. And I suppose it had a lot to do with the way that the family turned out, that the boys turned out to be...pretty tough kids. I suppose he has to take his share of the responsibility for what happened to his family."

—GENE HACKMAN (NICHOLAS EARP)

I've been a huge Hackman fan for twenty-five years, since *Bonnie and Clyde*. I've seen most of his movies, and he is always spectacularly true and forceful. I don't think he can act falsely. I

needed someone with that kind of bearing and stature to be the patriarch of this family, that spawned these brothers. Someone who has that sort of force about him, weight.

"He has one of the great faces ever, a face, just like you'd see in a pictorial history of the Civil War. It's a joy to photograph it. When he came to get wardrobed, he had this beard he'd grown for another movie, and it was terrific. And his instinct was exactly the same as mine, which was, since we were filming the part [of the film in which Nicholas is older] first, he should keep the beard for that and shave it for the younger part. With the beard he looks like a biblical elder. He's always had this incredible masculinity and vitality, but at the same time he's always been the most sensitive of actors. The thing that's distinguished his career is to be this big bear of a man who could be sensitive to the smallest things, play the most sensitive roles. It's a great combination for the wise father.

"Wyatt's whole life is a sort of working out of what his father and his mother have taught him, and some of the ideas that they've given him are hard to carry through on in the real world. But with someone as powerful as Gene, you understand the kind of impression a father could make on his son."

—LAWRENCE KASDAN

WYATT
Eighty acres of corn.

NICHOLAS
You take on a job, you finish it. A man who can't be depended on steady isn't worth the trouble of havin' around.

WYATT
(nods, frowning)
Why do you think they're comin' home soon, Pa?

NICHOLAS
This damn war can't last forever. Besides, that's what I want to happen.

Silence, except for the steady hoof-falls. Finally—

NICHOLAS
You know I'm gonna have to whup you a bit.

Wyatt nods.

EXT. EARP FARMHOUSE—NIGHT
Middle of the night. Wyatt, in a nightshirt,

with a Springfield rifle in his hands, walks out into the front yard and stops. He looks around at the moonlit farmland, then focuses on the carbine in his hands. He weighs and balances it lovingly, then hoists it smoothly to his shoulder, sighting off across the fields. He follows an imaginary moving target and fires off an imaginary round, making the sound of a shot. He loves the feel of the thing in his grasp.

The boy lowers the gun, leans it on his shoulder, soldier-style, and marches across the moonlit space. He stops dramatically, brings the rifle down in readiness in front of his chest and breaks at a run toward a nearby corral, hearing the commencement of some skirmish in his head.

Wyatt scales the fence with animal grace, fires off another imaginary round from the top rail, and jumps down into the corral. The two heavy farm horses there give him a curious look. He moves by them stealthily, then uses the fence at the other side to steady his aim at some phantom advancing force.

> WYATT
> (a whisper)
> Come on, Johnny Reb.

Ian Bohen as Young Wyatt

He peers down the sight for a moment, then suddenly swings the barrel up and around to a new target—

The moon. It hangs white and fat in the Iowa night. Wyatt plugs it—once, twice, three times. Then there is only QUIET.

Wyatt stares at the moon as though he expects it to fall. After a moment, he HEARS the SQUEAK AND CREAK OF A WAGON. Wyatt whips around in surprise, peering off toward the entry road.

A BUCKBOARD WAGON is approaching the farmhouse, ghostly in the half-light, a lone driver on the seat.

Wyatt squints to make out the figure. He can't quite believe what he's seeing.

> WYATT
> Virgil?

The wagon pulls into the front of the farmhouse as Wyatt comes running up, shouting now—

> WYATT
> Virgil!

VIRGIL EARP (20) climbs wearily down from the wagon and faces Wyatt. They look each other over for a moment—they've both changed a lot. Then Virgil opens his arms and takes his brother in his embrace.

> VIRGIL
> Look who got long and tall.

> WYATT
> We didn't know you was comin'. Why didn't you send word?

> VIRGIL
> We didn't know ourselves. Then we thought we should just come on.

> WYATT
> Is James comin' too?

A look crosses Virgil's face. He forces a smile.

> VIRGIL
> Why, James is right here with me, Wyatt.

Virgil leads Wyatt around to the rear of the wagon and lowers the back. There, almost unidentifiable at first among a jumble of grain bags, saddles, and bedrolls, in what amounts to a jerry-built ambulance, lies JAMES EARP (22).

He is awake and smiling now at Wyatt, but he doesn't look good. He is deathly thin, his face

streaked with permanent pain lines. He could be ten years older. Wyatt is shocked by his appearance.

> JAMES
> Hey, Wyatt. Don't shoot me now, ya hear.

Wyatt looks down, surprised to find the rifle still in his hands. He feels suddenly ashamed.

> WYATT
> James…James, welcome home.

> VIRGIL
> (climbing up on the wagon)
> Come on, boy, give us a hand here.

ON THE PORCH. Nicholas Earp comes out the front door in his night clothes, awakened by the voices. He stops in his tracks as he sees Virgil and Wyatt help the horribly injured James down off the wagon. One arm is bound tightly to his body under his clothes and he appears all crooked. Each movement causes him pain. Once on the ground, Wyatt steadies him, but James insists on taking a crutch and

hobbling forward on his on steam. It seems an act of pure heroism.

James looks up from his struggles to see his father watching from the front porch. Virgil sees him too and there is great joy here, despite everything. The two returning vets move slowly to meet Nicholas, who comes to them from the porch.

Wyatt stays behind, watching James's struggle. There are tears in his eyes.

INT. FRONT ROOM, EARP FARM-
HOUSE—DAY
Start CLOSE ON Nicholas at the head of the long dinner table, SLOWLY PULLING BACK to reveal the entire Earp family—the only time we'll see them all together—at supper. Wyatt is holding the baby ADELIA on his lap and feeding her. Wyatt's sister MARTHA (18) is here. VIRGINIA, Wyatt's mother, moves about the table throughout this action, and her reactions are clear. There is a lovely, clear openness between her and her husband, no intimidation. They're a lively combination.

NICHOLAS
When your mother and I were married
back in Kentucky, she didn't count on
being moved around like a travelin' tent
show. But she went with me to Illinois
without complaint. And when I brought
her here to Iowa, she remained tolerant.
Your mother believes that there is something wrong with me. She says there is
something in my blood that will not
allow me to stay put. Well, she may be
right. If she's lucky, I haven't passed it on
to you. Time will tell. But for this family,
the time has come to move on again. To
the west of here is a vast expanse of
untamed territory, full of wild Indians
and countless dangers. But beyond that
wilderness lies a land of great promise,
where civilization has flourished for hundreds of years. We'll go to California and
see what we can make of that place.

We can see the length of the table now, and
this news has differing effects on the children
old enough to understand.

MARTHA
But why, Pa?

NICHOLAS
There is opportunity for lawyers out
there and there is still rich land available
to people who know how to work. In
California, Wyatt will study the law and,
perhaps, come to work with me.
    (his eyes smile)
Maybe Morgan and Warren will join our
firm.

WYATT
And Adelia, too, I guess.

There is general laughter.

VIRGINIA
That's right, don't forget the baby. Everybody's got to work.

6

VIRGIL
I've told Pa I'm not going. I want to see what's available to me here. I'll join you later if things don't work out.

MARTHA
I don't want to go, either.

MORGAN
(to James and Virgil)
Martha's in love with Jimmy Jorgenson!

She shoots her brother a killing look.

JAMES
Good for you, Martha. He's a stand-up boy.

VIRGINIA
That's right. And his family knows what it means to put down roots.
(she throws a look at Nicholas)
Martha, if you don't want to go, that's your decision.

Martha is a little shocked, but she starts to get used to the idea pretty fast.

NICHOLAS
James has decided to come along with us. Which suits me fine. The closer you can keep your family, the better. They're the only ones you can rely on.
(he leans forward, dramatically)
Remember this, all of you, nothing counts so much as blood. The rest are just strangers.

This plunges the room into its first true silence. Finally—

VIRGINIA
You already told them that, Nicholas.

JAMES
…A hundred times…

NICHOLAS
…Can't hear it enough…

VIRGIL
…A thousand times…

The whole family begins to laugh—except for Nicholas, who struggles to maintain his stern countenance.

WARREN
I heard ya, Pa! Blood counts the most!

The laughter grows. A smile splits Nicholas's face as he pretends to backhand little Warren.

WYATT
(holding her up)
Tell the baby, Pa. She ain't heard.

EXT. ROLLING COUNTRY—DAY
Lovely Midwestern landscape. Scattered trees and low brush dot the hills. No one in sight; just great open, empty land.

Now a rider appears over a rise at a gentle lope. It is Wyatt. Tied to the rump of his horse is the fresh carcass of an antelope. He rides past.

REVERSE. Wyatt heads down the slope into a long valley. Stretching into the distance is a WAGON TRAIN. There are twenty wagons and buckboards, single riders on horseback, and, at the rear, cattle, oxen, and horses.

EXT. OUTSKIRTS OF OMAHA, NEBRASKA—DAY
The wagon train has stopped outside the flimsy settlement of Omaha, a couple of streets, a lot of tents and corrals. It can be seen in the distance, and what substance it has is derived from the large transient population which has converged on this jumping-off point for the Overland Trail.

TOM CHAPMAN has pulled a buckboard up near the Earp wagon and waits as Wyatt stands by the tailgate looking in at his mother. She looks for one more thing, makes a notation on some paper in her hand and gives it to Wyatt.

VIRGINIA
Just get the things and get back. Don't talk to anyone you don't have business with.

CHAPMAN
Don't you worry, Miz Earp, I'll keep an eye on him.

Wyatt shoots him a look.

VIRGINIA
That doesn't comfort me, Tom Chapman. Both of you, use your heads. And don't linger!

"TO THE WEST OF HERE IS A VAST EXPANSE OF UNTAMED TERRITORY..."

"One of the ideas of the movie is that when Nicholas tells his family that they're moving to California, he describes it as them moving from civilization in the Midwest to a civilization in California. In between is untamed land. And they'll travel through the dangers of that untamed land. But the idea is to get to civilization. What happens to Wyatt and his brothers is that they get stuck in the middle and what we see in this section of the movie is Young Wyatt falling in love with these wide-open spaces. The very wildness that Nicholas is worried about is the thing that attracts Wyatt, and he spends the rest of his life wandering through that wildness."

— LAWRENCE KASDAN

Wyatt flashes Chapman a secret grin as he climbs up on the wagon.

>   WYATT
> Don't you worry, Ma. We won't shame
> ya.

Chapman gets the wagon moving, a little too fast, and they head for town.

EXT. MAIN STREET, OMAHA—DAY
The street is teeming with activity. Merchants, travelers of every description, townfolk, freighters and bullwhackers. Wagons clog the thoroughfare. Dogs and children dart about. Lots of dust.

Wyatt brings a heavy sack out of a store and uses his whole weight to flop it into the buckboard. He wipes his brow and examines the list he has pulled from his pocket. He looks across the road.

Chapman is standing next to a wagon, talking up to a Mormon Girl, passably pretty given the environment. At that moment her Father, a fearsome-looking Elder, walks up carrying a newly purchased pitchfork. The girl shrinks back into the wagon. Chapman turns his usual smile on the Elder and extends his hand. The Elder gives Chapman a glare of such intensity that the boy finally just shrinks away, with one farewell glance at the girl.

Wyatt laughs as his friend rejoins him and they head off down the sidewalk.

EXT. SALOON/ STREET—DAY
The two boys have to pick their way through the crowds on the wooden sidewalk. As they are about to pass the doors of the saloon, Chapman indicates that they ought to stop in and tip a few. Wyatt has barely begun to demur when there is a sudden flood of bodies out the doors of the saloon, sweeping away everything in its path. Thirty men come pouring out into the street. It becomes immediately clear from the flow of the crowd that two of the men, a Short Bullwhacker and a Dirty Sodbuster, are having a heated disagreement. Their words are lost in the din of the street, but the action has now grabbed the attention of everyone in the vicinity. The crowd of men around the combatants closes in a circle, expecting fisticuffs, but after a few more vocifer-

ous exchanges, the Short Bullwhacker puts his hand emphatically on the butt of the old Army pistol stuck in his pants. The Dirty Sodbuster immediately begins the slow process of extracting a revolver from a cumbersome belt he wears awkwardly at his side. The two men reflexively back away from each other.

With that, the waters part and the crowd shrinks back in a panic. Down the street in each direction, people scurry for cover in a widening wave, parents rush to pull their children from the street.

Wyatt and Chapman are fairly slammed against the front of the saloon in the crush of bodies, but their gaze never leaves the street.

It is all happening very fast now. A friend of the Short Bullwhacker makes a final entreaty for him to call it off, but hits the dirt as he sees it's already a done thing. The two slow gunmen have each cleared their weapons and, at a distance of about 15 feet, immediately begin to fire as fast as they can manage. The Short Bullwhacker gets off three shots, the Dirty Sodbuster two. The sound of the guns is DEAFENING. SCREAMS OF ALARM fill the road.

Wyatt flinches with each shot, watching in horror. He's never seen guns aimed at people.

It's over in seconds. Both men are down. One squirms in agony, the other is still. The crowd, Chapman among them, surges back into the street to surround the men.

DOWN THE BLOCK, a horse lies in the dust, victim of a stray bullet, its legs kicking in death throes. Its owner holds his head in disbelief. Wyatt stands where he is, his face drained of blood, staring.

WYATT'S POV. Through a momentary gap in the crowd, the Dirty Sodbuster can be seen jerking in the dust, a huge circle of blood staining his pants from the groin outward.

Wyatt suddenly feels sick and turns in a panic, looking for somewhere to go.

AROUND THE CORNER of the building, not even an alley, just an inset, Wyatt lurches up to the wall and is sick behind some barrels.

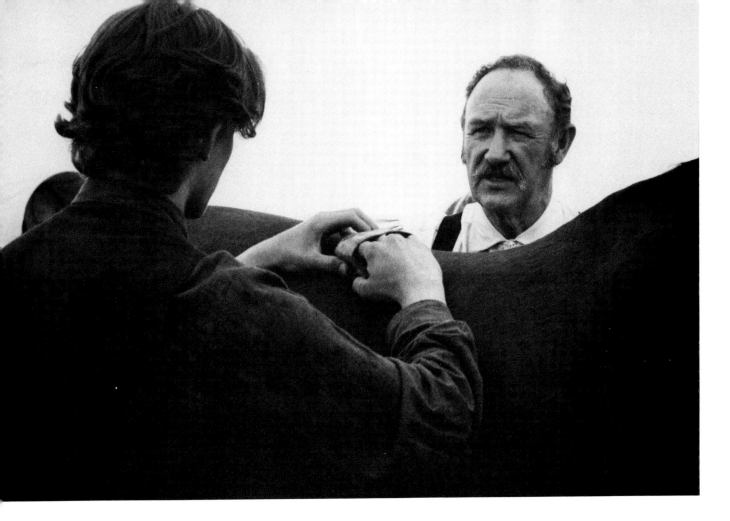

EXT. WAGON TRAIN, OUTSKIRTS OF
OMAHA—NIGHT
Wyatt is tending to the horses tied in a group to
picket lines. He brushes their coats and cleans
and checks the hooves. At a distance around
the makeshift corral, other men and boys feed
and groom the stock.

Nicholas appears from the direction of the wagons and stands watching his son for a few moments. He relights his pipe.

> NICHOLAS
> How you doing, Wyatt?

> WYATT
> I'm okay, Pa.

> NICHOLAS
> This land is full of people doing wicked
> things to each other.

> WYATT
> I ain't afraid. I like it out here. I like how
> nothing much has been touched.

> NICHOLAS
> I've got to tell you something, Wyatt. I told
> your brothers when they went off to fight
> and I suppose the time has come for you.
> (he looks off into the night)
> You know I'm a man who believes in the
> law. After your family, it's about all we
> got to believe in.
> (Wyatt acknowledges that)
> But there are plenty of men who don't
> care about the law. Men who will take
> part in any kind of viciousness and not
> care who gets hurt. In fact, the more that
> get hurt, the better. When you find your-
> self in a fight with such viciousness…
> (he pauses, looks at Wyatt)
> …hit first, if you can. And when you do
> hit…hit to kill.

Wyatt is surprised, but he tries not to show it.
He meets his father's gaze and there is a question in the boy's eyes.

> NICHOLAS
> You'll know. Don't worry, you'll know
> when it's come to that.

11

Nicholas turns and walks back toward the wagons. He speaks over his shoulder.

> NICHOLAS
> The Earps always know.

EXT. WYOMING PLAINS—DAY
The wagon train is tiny in the distance as it crosses an immense, rolling plain.

EXT. MOJAVE DESERT—DAY
Blinding light. A cloud of dust blows violently past camera. When it clears, we see the wagon train circled and sitting oddly still for the daylight hours. The WIND howls and whips at the wagon covers. Dust swirls everywhere.

At one of the wagons, the mother of the family reaches through the back sheeting to pull it even tighter against the wind.

At another wagon, the family dog peeks out the side and HOWLS a reply to the wind.

INT. SECOND EARP WAGON—DAY
Inside the cramped wagon, Virginia works repairing some clothing. Behind her, James takes a surreptitious swig from his flask. Adelia totters over the packing, cranky. The WIND beats the wagon cover into an incessant SNAPPING SOUND.

INT. FIRST EARP WAGON—DAY
Nicholas is reading a book. He looks up once at the whipping cover and wipes his eyes of dust. Warren fiddles with a crude toy.

EXT. PICKET LINE CORRAL—DAY
The horses and oxen are suffering in the heat and the wind, spooky and restless.

Wyatt is out here among them. (Other men are dimly seen in the dust, tending their animals.) Wyatt is bundled against the wind, his face wrapped in cloth, with an opening only for his eyes. He ties a line and calms a mare, then bends under the line and walks out toward the open desert. He resembles an Arab as he stands looking at the swirling sands.

CU* Wyatt's eyes. He may be the only living creature in the vicinity who is perfectly happy.

EXT. MOJAVE DESERT—NIGHT
The wagon train crosses this hottest stretch of

the trip at night. The flat terrain is lit by a full moon; it looks more like an eerie day. It is very quiet. The CREAK and WHINE of the wagons, the SHUFFLE of hooves the only sounds.

Wyatt is driving the first Earp wagon at the front of the train. His mother sits next to him on the seat.

> WYATT
> Mr. Thorsen says he knows a man in San Berdoo who might need drivers. They haul freight all over the territory. Mr. Thorsen thinks I'm good enough to do the job.

> VIRGINIA
> Mr. Thorsen is mighty helpful about things that are none of his business. You better not tell your father how helpful Mr. Thorsen is being.

> WYATT
> I guess Pa won't like the idea much.

Virginia throws him a small smile.

> WYATT
> I could put off studying the law a while, I figure. There's plenty of time for that later.

> VIRGINIA
> Yes, there's time for that later.

> WYATT
> I suppose Pa won't see it that way.

> VIRGINIA
> If your father wanted sons that would do just what he told them, he should have raised them different. The thing you all learned from your father is you have to do what your heart tells you, no matter what anybody else says.

> WYATT
> (looks at her)
> I didn't learn that from *Pa*.

She gives him a warm look and touches his hair. Wyatt gazes out across the desert ahead.

> VIRGINIA
> I believe you're the only person on this train that wishes this trip weren't ever going to end.

*Close-up.

12

WYATT'S POV. Over the heads of the oxen, moving into the otherworldly landscape ahead, the dark outline of mountains in the distance.

> WYATT
> I didn't expect it, Ma…but this is the best place I been.

CLOSE ON a side view of the WAGON WHEELS as they slowly roll RIGHT TO LEFT through the desert dust in the gloom. We begin a—

LONG, SLOW MATCHED DISSOLVE TO: CLOSE ON a side view of different WHEELS, those of a big freight wagon, rolling FAST AND BUMPY over rough road LEFT TO RIGHT. We hang on them several beats as the bright sunlight of our new setting floods the screen, then the CAMERA MOVES UP AND BEHIND the wildly speeding wagon. We hear plenty of GUNFIRE. We are—

EXT. CANYON ROAD, WYOMING (1869)—DAY
We're up the back of the overloaded wagon now, looking forward. The wagon, drawn by a dozen big horses, is hurtling down a rough road in rocky country. There is a stubbled fellow in his thirties, DUTCH WILEY, stretched out over the cargo in the wagon, firing a Winchester rifle back at us.

REVERSE ANGLE. Four Highwaymen are chasing the wagon and firing intermittent shots. They must not have calculated this holdup perfectly because they're desperately playing catch-up right now.

One of their shots hits the cargo close to Dutch and he recoils. He's mad as much as frightened. He yells down over his shoulder to the wagon's driver, whom we haven't seen yet.

> DUTCH WILEY
> Dammit, Wyatt! Move this wagon! They're catchin' up!

"…FULL OF COUNTLESS DANGERS."

I wanted to pick Wyatt's life up again at a time when he's hauling freight for the railway camps that were building the transcontinental railroad. And [the wagon chase] seemed like a good way to get into that. It was a very dangerous job. They were constantly accosted by highwaymen. Their freight was valuable. And it took enormous courage to do that job. It was a very adventuresome, vigorous life that attracted young men.

"I had a lot of concerns because it's very dangerous stunt work. The wagon is going full speed down the canyon road with an actor/stuntman on top. It could have flipped over at any time and both men are totally vulnerable. We prepared the sequence for a month, carefully thought out how the wagon should be constructed and weighted. The horses had to be trained to go that fast on that kind of road pulling that big a load. It all worked out great, it was an auspicious start to a difficult production. The cut sequence is very exciting and it's not manufactured. It really is an exciting stunt." —LAWRENCE KASDAN

The biggest stunt sequence in the movie was the freight wagon chase, because that's something that has never been done like that—coming down that canyon, with the drop-off on each side and the horses running as fast as they were. Usually when you see chases, it's pretty controlled, but we wanted the audience to feel the speed. I think it comes across. We worked three weeks, every day, prepping that. In addition to working the horses and distributing the weight of the wagon, we had to grade the road for traction. There was a lot to that scene."
—NORM HOWELL, STUNT COORDINATOR

The scene that had the most room for something to go wrong was the freight wagon chase. That was where you could get somebody hurt or you could have a wreck, tear something up, hurt horses.

"We figured that we had to have two sets of six horses. We had two horses that looked alike in each position, so that was twelve horses that not only had to match, but also had to be able to pull a wagon. Not all horses can do that.

"We started them off at a walk, then taught them to run. Then we worked the other team. The two teams couldn't really cross over, because once you really chase a team, once they chase and chase and chase, that's all they want to do—run. Since we had a lot of slow sequences, we wanted to have a fast team and a quiet team. We tried to use the runners for the running and the others for the dialogue scenes and standing still and for Kevin to drive into town. We didn't run the quiet team at all, so they were very solid. For me, that's a great thing to see—an actor driving a six-up [six-horse team]. You don't see that much [this is almost always the type of work reserved for a stuntman or wrangler]. To be able to see Kevin drive, all the work was worth it."—RUSTY HENDRICKSON, HEAD WRANGLER

WYATT (OS)*
This is all we got, Dutch!

DUTCH WILEY
(firing again)
Well, whip those nags, you bastard! And quit laughin', cause we're pretty close to dead!

CUT TO THE DRIVER. For the first time in the movie we see the man (Kevin Costner) we're going to take this journey with: WYATT EARP at 21 years of age. And damn if he doesn't seem to be finishing a laugh right now. Not because the danger isn't real, not because he's ready to die, not because he's an idiot. Just because he's driving that team so well and the whole death-defying enterprise is moving so fast

through the rocks, he can't really control the feeling it gives him. If he's going to die, which he has no intention of doing right now, it might just as well be laughing. A bullet tears off a chunk of the wagon near Wyatt. The remaining smile is gone.

DUTCH WILEY
They're on us now!

WYATT
Shoot the horse!

DUTCH WILEY
What?

WYATT
Shoot the lead horse! You can hit a horse, can't you?

*Off screen

14

Dutch takes careful aim at the nearest Highwayman, who fires again at Dutch. Dutch shoots the horse and they go down in an ugly wreck. The other three Highwaymen fly past their partner on momentum, but they suddenly have lost their desire. Dutch fires at the second man. Raggedly, all three remaining Highwaymen pull up and begin to recede in the distance.

EXT. FOOTHILLS, WYOMING—DAY
The wagon is stopped on the road out of the hills. The great plains open up below them. Wyatt and Dutch finish re-tying the freight that's been jostled and climb up onto the wagon. They're slow to start talking. Finally—

> DUTCH WILEY
> That horse never did nothin' to me.

Wyatt nods. He's feeling a little down, too.

> DUTCH WILEY
> You should be ridin' shotgun. I seen you shoot.
>   (Wyatt is silent)
> 'Course I can't handle the team like you…
>   (he looks off across the plain)
> Ah hell, we made it. That's the thing.

They're quiet for a while.

WYATT
You ever shoot a man, Dutch?

DUTCH WILEY
Sure…I shot a few. How ya think I got this job?

They both know he's lying.

DUTCH WILEY
How 'bout yourself ?

WYATT
Nope. Hope I never do, either.

DUTCH WILEY
Good luck.

EXT. GREAT PLAINS, WYOMING—DAY
CLOSE ON a railroad tie being laid into place on a freshly graded bed of earth. A length of fresh rail is laid upon it. BODIES SWARM between CAMERA and railroad track as the incredibly efficient track-laying of the Intercontinental Railroad proceeds through this section of Wyoming.

WE'RE PULLING UP AND BACK NOW to see the incredible beehive of activity as the track moves west. There are hundreds of Workers (mostly Chinese) and Foremen and Drivers and Haulers—all the massed skill and energy and strength required to move the thin strip of Iron Road across the nation. The new track arrives here from around a rise in the distance.

Wyatt and Dutch join a parade of wagons on a newly created road that leads to the bustling Railway Camp up ahead of the advancing track.

EXT. WYATT'S WAGON, ROAD INTO RAILWAY CAMP—DAY
Dutch is looking up ahead at the Railway

Camp. Wyatt is focused on the crew laying the track. He seems fascinated by the activity.

> DUTCH WILEY
> I'm gonna get drunk, win a fortune, and find the best woman money can buy. Then I'm gonna sleep for two days.

A Rider named RED comes up the road from the opposite direction. When he sees them he pulls up beside to ride along.

> RED
> (friendly)
> Well, if it ain't the sore-ass boys, back for another visit on the fourth of July. I hope you got some sugar in that load. I ain't had no real sugar for a month.

> WYATT
> Red.

> DUTCH WILEY
> What's happening in this hellhole, Red? Any new ladies up to my standards?

> RED
> I believe there is a new one just perfect for you, Dutch. She can stay awake two minutes at a time and she favors tiny little wangers.
> (Wyatt laughs)
> Prize fight Sunday morning, Wyatt. Ya gonna referee?

> WYATT
> Last time some of the boys didn't like the decision.

> RED
> (wheeling his horse to take off)
> To hell with them. Sore losers!

He rides away as the wagon continues into town.

EXT. MAIN DRAG, RAILWAY CAMP— DAY

Wyatt's wagon pulls into the camp. There are only a few wooden structures here, mainly saloons. Most of the temporary town is made up of tents of every description. But all the services of a normal town are provided from those establishments. It's a rough and raucous place, buzzing with activity and unfocused energy. The only women in town are prostitutes and a few stout-hearted entrepreneurs, several of whom greet Wyatt and Dutch by name, as do many of the men.

Wyatt looks comfortable here. He thinks it's the greatest show on earth.

WIPE TO:
EXT. CLEARING AMONG THE TENTS—DAY
SUNDAY MORNING, THE FOURTH OF JULY. There are several hundred people gathered to witness a prize fight between young JOHN SHANSSEY and the older, more experienced Mike Donovan. Donovan is on his way to a professional boxing career. Shanssey is on his way to a career as a barkeep (and mayor of Yuma, Arizona). He's game, but he's getting the worst of it. A rough attempt has been made to festoon the ring area with patriotic bunting and decorations.

Wyatt is in the ring too, crisply refereeing. He knows what he's doing and moves like a boxer himself.

Shanssey absorbs a devastating onslaught like the tough young man he is, but finally is knocked to the canvas by a surprise left. Wyatt begins the count as Shanssey struggles to his feet. The fight resumes, but Donovan puts him down again. When Shanssey, operating only on grit and pride, uses the ropes to get up again, Wyatt stops the fight. Shanssey collapses into his arms, bloody.

> SHANSSEY
> (gasping, to Wyatt only)
> …God bless you…

A FEW MINUTES LATER. Wyatt and Dutch are making their way through the departing crowd. A big, unpleasant-looking gambler, ROSS, puts a rough hand on Wyatt's arm and turns him. Ross has several friends with him.

> ROSS
> You don't know a boxing ring from a mule's asshole. And you've *twice* cost me money.

Wyatt doesn't know this guy or what his gripe is.

> WYATT
> Sorry you didn't like—

IDA RANDOM, PRODUCTION DESIGNER

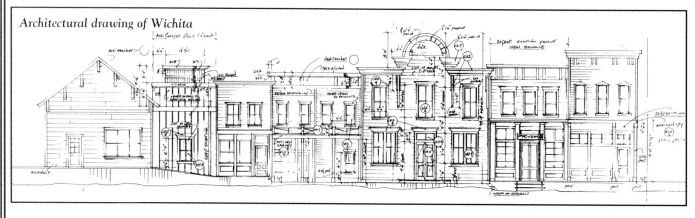

Architectural drawing of Wichita

ON HER PREPARATION FOR *WYATT EARP*

Y ou have to know what the film's going to look like before you start. You have to have a plan, especially on a picture this size. I spent quite a while in the beginning making what I call 'concept boards.' At first I took weeks just gathering all the research—accumulating pictures, wallpaper and color samples. From that research, I pulled what I wanted to use and made color xeroxes. I made concept boards for all the major sets. This process is one of the most important things I do before the movie begins. For example, there are ten or eleven saloons in the movie, and each saloon has a different look. So I made boards for all the major saloons, just to start organizing ideas. Then I showed those boards to Larry, and that's how we decided what these saloons were going to look like. This is one way you communicate your ideas visually to the director and all the other departments. You can tell them what it's going to look like, but people like to see things."

USING TWO "TOWN" SETS TO POR-TRAY EIGHT DIFFERENT TOWNS

O ne of the keys to this trick is deciding exactly what you're going to show in what town. You just have to limit your shots. You have to go and look, take pictures, and decide, 'This is where the camera's going to be and this is what we're going to see in this town.' Also, I had different color schemes for each town. I kept all the sandy colors in Wichita, and all the burnished colors in Tombstone. When we got to Dodge City,

which was mostly night shooting, I used a lot of cool colors like greens and blues—night colors. The difference in color helps change the looks for the separate towns.

"After that, we altered the existing facades—new fronts, porches, details, different windows. Then, of course, we changed all the street decorations, from lighting fixtures to window dressing. The use of tents also helped define the different towns. For example, I saw in the research that mining towns like Tombstone had large tent communities while cattle towns like Dodge and Wichita had very few."

Detail from the Comique Theater and Saloon

PRODUCTION DESIGN

A ll of the designer's work is for the frame. It's like a painting. *Wyatt Earp* was shot in anamorphic. [*Anamorphic refers to the technology that makes possible the wide-screen format used on* Wyatt Earp. *The alternate format, often referred to as "standard," has a shorter width relative to the height of the frame.*] When you are building sets and shooting in such a wide format, you find elements that fill the frame and make it more interesting. You become very conscious of the details—door frames, door jambs, fireplace lines, how high, how low, etc. I think designers have to pay a lot of attention to what is in the camera's eye, what the camera sees. Because that's all there is."

ON *WYATT EARP*

W hen I first read the script, I was reading the story. But after the fifth saloon, all I could see were saloons. There was the sixth, seventh, and eighth saloon—and more—I just couldn't believe it. It was so much movie that I stopped reading the story and started reading the sets, just to know how big it actually was. Then I re-read the script for the story. Ninety-three, ninety-four sets—you know automatically most sets will have to be built because you can't go out and find practical [existing] sets of the Old West.

"It's very interesting to do Westerns because although the buildings were pretty simplistic on the outside, the inside of many buildings were filled with all sorts of interior veneers and ornamentation—carved wooden bars, pressed metal ceilings, and exquisite wallpaper and furnishings. That made it fun for Cheryl

Carasik [Set Decorator] and me to decorate the sets.

"Doing *Wyatt Earp* was a real joy, which is a great thing to be able to say. A lot of it comes from Larry, just from who he is and how it is to work with him. It's just such a comfortable relationship. Although the work is hard, we laugh and we have a good time. I really feel close to him."

KASDAN ON RANDOM

This is our third movie together. Ida designed *The Big Chill* and *Silverado*, too. And [the success of the relationship] really has to do with communicating clearly with each other, and then having someone whose taste and aesthetic are congenial to yours. And I trust her taste implicitly. She knows what to ask me, she knows what I'm going to like, she knows a lot of things from working with me over three pictures. I loved the job she did on *Silverado*, so I was excited about her doing another Western. When she did *Silverado*, that was far and away the biggest picture she'd ever been near as a designer. Now she's done a lot of big pictures and had a lot of success and her confidence has grown. So you take this wonderful taste she has, add it to a lot of experience, and she's just one of the top people there is.

"Ida's very sensitive to the narrative, to the thematic material. She relates to the script strongly in that way initially. She has a highly refined aesthetic and I trust it enormously. In fact, that was the thing I loved about her work on *The Big Chill*, way back. I just thought her taste was impeccable. Very imaginative, too. Her mind works in unusual ways and with that you get the surprising detail, the surprising concept, the surprising grand plan. That's what you're looking for."

Ross suddenly punches Wyatt, sending him down. Dutch makes a move toward Ross, but the gambler's friends heave him back into the crowd. Ross is already gone and his friends follow.

Wyatt sits in the dirt, more surprised than hurt. People offer their hands, but he's in no hurry to get up. He gazes off in the direction Ross has disappeared and rubs his jaw.

INT. LUCKY'S SALOON—NIGHT
The place is large and crowded, wild and loud. There are all the games of chance, pool tables, long rough-hewn bar, etc.

Wyatt stands near a Faro table, which is crowded with players. Attached to his arm and gently stroking his sore jaw is a prostitute named SALLY, though Wyatt seems entirely preoccupied with the Faro game, which is new to him. He's jokey and familiar with the girl; they've done this dance before.

WYATT
…This is the damndest game I ever saw.

SALLY
You can't get a spot now anyway, Wyatt. Why don't you come with me for a while?

WYATT
(his eyes never leave the game)
I just don't know if that'd be the right thing to do, Sally. You see, I've promised my heart to another.

SALLY
(looks around)
Which girl? I'll fight her for you.

WYATT
Oh, it's no one here. She's back in Lamar, Missouri, where my grandparents live.

SALLY
Missouri! She ain't gonna help you tonight. And she sure won't know nothin' 'bout what we do here.

WYATT
Oh, Urilla doesn't even know about our great love. I haven't seen her for six years. But I'm going back to Missouri soon and tell her.

SALLY
Urilla? That's a silly kind of name. How can you promise your heart to someone who don't even know about it?

WYATT
(indicating one of the players)
What's that fellow doing? He's winning all the time. I think Urilla's a pretty name. But not as pretty as she is. I saw her three times back in '63 and the third time she smiled at me just right.

SALLY
I guarantee you she don't know what I know.

WYATT
(laughs)
I bet you're right about that.' Less things have changed in Lamar…

Red, whom Wyatt saw on the road into town, walks up.

RED
Wyatt, your boy Dutch is drunk and tellin' everybody how you're gonna take Ed Ross.

WYATT
Damn. Who the hell is Ed Ross?

RED
He's the guy who decked you this morning at the fight. I'd get ahold of Dutch before he starts some real trouble for ya.

SALLY
I know Ed Ross…he's bad business.

WYATT
I better find Dutch.

A Player gets up from the Faro table and indicates the seat is open to Wyatt. He looks around a moment, torn, then sits down.

WYATT
(to Dealer)
How do you play this game?

DEALER
Simple, friend. Place your bet by the number you think is a winner. If you're bettin' for it to lose, copper it with a penny on top.

Wyatt puts one chip down on the Ace as the other players place their bets. The Dealer pulls a card from the box and places it face-up on the table. It's a Nine. Wyatt frowns.

DEALER
That's the Loser, you're still in.

The Dealer takes the next card, the Winner, from the box and shows it— an Ace. He places another chip on top of Wyatt's and settles with the other bettors. Wyatt is delighted as he pulls in his winnings.

WYATT
I had a feeling this was the game for me.

Wyatt places three chips on the Jack. The Dealer plays another turn and Wyatt wins again. Now he's really getting excited. Sally likes it too.

WYATT
(to Sally)
Now, could we have a better time than this upstairs?

SALLY
At least upstairs I'd be makin' some money.

WYATT
You might get it yet.

ROSS (OS)
(loud and mean)
Wyatt Earp!

Ross is standing fifteen feet away. His coat is pulled back behind a holstered Colt .44 army revolver. His tone is clear enough to QUIET the room. Bystanders quickly move out of the way. Even the Dealer moves swiftly from his post. Wyatt has never been in this situation before. He's a little slow to get the full import of what's happening. He gets up from his chair and turns around. We see for the first time that he has an old Army pistol stuck in his pants, in a way that shows he's never had to draw it in anger (or haste). Turning has brought him up against a pool table, between him and Ross, its players scattered now.

WYATT
That's my name.

ROSS
Well, it don't mean shit to me or any-body else in this world. And it never will after this night.

SALLY
Ed, this boy ain't worth your trouble…

ROSS
Shut up, Sally! You and I are gonna talk later. Earp, I heard you were lookin' for me to make a fight…so I thought I'd be easy to find.

WYATT
You heard wrong, mister. The only thing that's happened between us is I got popped good. I don't want to—

21

ROSS
Stop talkin'!

WYATT
(quiet)
Okay.

As Ross begins to set himself for the draw, Wyatt does something that surprises everyone in the room, maybe including him. He reaches down and picks up the cue ball from the pool table in front of him. Before anyone realizes what he's doing, he has taken it back and heaved it with tremendous force at Ross.

The ball hits Ross in the center of his chest while his hand is still reaching for his gun. He flies backward with a surprised look on his face, banging hard against the bar as he goes down. He winds up on his back, head crooked against the base of the bar, his eyes askew, making CHOKING, GURGLING NOISES. He cannot begin to move.

Everyone in the room is shocked. This is something new.

WYATT'S FACE. He stares at the fallen man. Something happens. *His face changes in some tiny way that no one would notice. But it changes.*

Wyatt walks over to Ross. As he does, he looks at the men in his path to see if anyone wants to take exception. He bends down and unbuckles Ross's gunbelt, then holds it up to the room.

WYATT
This man wanted to shoot me down…
over nothing. He lost. I'm taking his gun.

With that, Wyatt takes the old Army pistol from his pants and drops it on the gasping Ross. He takes the handsome holster and STRAPS IT ON HIS HIP FOR THE FIRST TIME. It looks natural, like it was always meant to be there.

Sally has crossed the room to his side. He takes her arm and walks out of the saloon. The room ERUPTS in chattering reaction.

EXT. STREET OUTSIDE LUCKY'S SALOON—NIGHT
Wyatt and Sally come out of the saloon. Wyatt walks a little differently with the holster on. They move out into the street.

Down at the end of the street in the distance, a crowd has gathered in a wide space. And now we see why—

With a LOUD RACKET primitive FIRE-WORKS erupt in the sky, lighting the Railway

Camp in red, white and blue bursts. The crowd down there reacts with pleasure.

Wyatt and Sally have stopped in the middle of the street to watch. Around them, all the hitched horses are shying and WHINNYING. Wyatt watches for a few moments, then looks down at his hip. His hand rests for a moment on the wooden butt of the Colt, then he grips it and draws the gun smoothly from the holster. Sally watches with curiosity as Wyatt weighs and balances the revolver in his hand, cocks and releases the hammer; he seems barely aware of her at the moment. Finally, he straightens his arm, aiming off in the distance, and slowly raises the barrel toward the exploding fireworks in the sky, just as he once aimed at the moon on the Iowa farm.

Wyatt's face, as he aims. He does not fire the weapon. He only makes the SOUND of a shot.

FIREWORKS, up there where Wyatt is aiming. After a red burst and a larger blue one, a huge white rocket erupts in the sky FILLING THE SCREEN WITH WHITE LIGHT as we— FADE TO WHITE.

FADE IN:
EXT. PRETTY NEIGHBORHOOD, LAMAR, MISSOURI (1870)—DAY
ON WYATT'S BACK as he walks down a sun-dappled street canopied with leafy trees. This street couldn't look more different from the rough dirt and dusty environs of the Railway Camp. Wyatt looks different too, even from the back. You'd have to call these clothes his Sunday Best. They're not just cleaner than what we've seen before, they're a touch more Eastern, citi-fied. Wyatt is carrying a bouquet of flowers. He turns up the walk to a pleasant house.

EXT. FRONT PORCH, SUTHERLAND HOUSE—DAY
Wyatt knocks on the door. It's answered by MRS. SUTHERLAND, a woman of fifty. She develops an inscrutable glimmer of a smile when she sees Wyatt.

MRS. SUTHERLAND
Yes?

WYATT
Hello, Mrs. Sutherland. I don't expect you'll remember me…

MRS. SUTHERLAND
I know perfectly well who you are, young man. Your grandmother told me you were coming back to Lamar.

WYATT
Yes, ma'am…I'm reading the law with Judge Earp.

MRS. SUTHERLAND
So I gathered.
(she looks him over)
You've changed a bit since your last visit. You do a fair impersonation of a grown man.

WYATT
Thank you, ma'am. I'm trying.

There is an extended moment of silence. It is awkward only for Wyatt. Mrs. Sutherland is toying with him.

MRS. SUTHERLAND
I'm not surprised to see you on my doorstep.

WYATT
No, ma'am?

MRS. SUTHERLAND
No. Are those flowers for me?

WYATT
If you would like them, then yes, they are.

He proffers the bouquet.

MRS. SUTHERLAND
No thanks.
(smiles, turning away)
Let me see if Urilla is around. She might take them.

She leaves him standing alone on the porch. He looks around the neighborhood, nervous.

URILLA SUTHERLAND comes out the front door. She is a blonde girl in her twenties, fresh and beautiful. Wyatt seems to have literally had his breath taken away; he can't speak for a moment. Urilla has lots of suitors, but she likes the way this one looks.

URILLA
Hello, Wyatt.

WYATT
Hello, Urilla.
(a long beat)
I brought you these.

"I SAW HER THREE TIMES BACK IN '63…"

I wanted Urilla to be completely open with no coyness to her. And I was struggling to find an actress who conveyed that. The hardest thing is to find the absolutely simple, clear approach to things.

"Annabeth [Gish] was the last woman we saw, but as soon as she read I knew that this was it. Because her face is the sun, just a source of light, and her way of reading was absolutely straightforward, a kind of idealized woman. And that's exactly what Wyatt has done with her—he's idealized her. He'd seen her when she was very young but he can't get over the idea of her. The image of her is so strong for him that it's more powerful than any reality. And Annabeth is a very attractive person. You can understand his infatuation. And she's very clear and simple, so you understand the charm of her. She represents some sort of perfect American woman to him, which is what he's after. And he's young. He thinks that all these things can be achieved. He believes that there's perfect virtue and you can live your life righteously and get away with it."
—LAWRENCE KASDAN

URILLA

Thank you.

(she takes the flowers and smells them)
I was glad when I heard you were coming back to town.

WYATT

You were?

URILLA

Yes, I was.

Wyatt is lost for a moment, distracted by the way the way she looks. He's quiet too long.

URILLA

What's wrong?

WYATT

Wrong?...Nothing...It's just that...

He lapses into silence.

URILLA

What is it, Wyatt?

WYATT

Well...I wasn't prepared for how beautiful you are.

Urilla blushes, pleased but not showing it much.

URILLA

Did you learn to talk that way out west?

Wyatt shakes his head "no." Urilla sits on a bench at the end of the porch and indicates that he should join her.

URILLA

So you've come to Lamar to study with your grandfather?

WYATT

Yes...and to marry you.

Urilla is taken aback. She gives him an embarrassed look, not sure she heard that right.

URILLA

Do you think it's as simple as that?

WYATT

No...I know it will take a great effort to win you. I know many men have tried. They failed because you were meant for me. But I will succeed. I'll begin today.

Urilla looks at him a long time. Then she begins to laugh. Soft and musical. It's a lovely sound.

EXT. FRONT PORCH, SUTHERLAND HOUSE—NIGHT
Only the golden light coming from the windows illuminate Wyatt and Urilla as he brings her home from a date. At the front door, he holds her very properly, but comfortably, in his arms and gives her their first goodnight kiss. It is almost chaste. When it is over, he releases her, but she continues to stand before him a long moment. Finally, she goes into the house.

EXT. FRONT YARD, SUTHERLAND HOUSE—DAY
Urilla sits on the back steps of the house doing some mending of her father's clothes. She wields the needle quickly, with that kind of aggressive skill that only real sewers possess. She's dressed like a farm girl, but she looks great. Wyatt thinks so. He's stretched out on the grass watching her.

URILLA

You know what they say about the Earps around here?

WYATT

Nope.

URILLA

They say old Judge Earp was the last one that could stay put. They say your father's got some kind of bug in his shoes...that if he isn't coming, he's going.

WYATT

There may be something to that. What else do they say?

URILLA

That it looks like his boys are the same way. No one knows where Virgil's gone and James has been on the move since the end of the War. They say that you won't likely...well, that's what they say.

WYATT

Is that what your father says?

URILLA

He agrees, I'll tell you that much.

WYATT

And why would any of that be of concern to your father?

URILLA
(he's caught her)
I don't know that it is. It's just talk, I
guess.

He watches her a moment. He knows he's making progress if they're debating it in the household.

WYATT
We know where everybody is. We always
keep in touch. That's one of my father's
rules. So they'll all be here.

URILLA
(looks up sharply, surprised)
Here? In Lamar? When?

He gives her his best smile.

WYATT
Why…for the wedding, of course.

She makes a face.

URILLA
Wyatt, you haven't learned the first thing
about playing "hard to get."
(he laughs)
A lot of girls would take advantage of a
fellow who made himself so available.

WYATT
I'm not interested in those girls.

She sews in silence for a few moments. Then,
never looking up—

URILLA
I don't ever want to leave my family,
Wyatt. I want to stay in this town and
get married and have lots of babies right
here in Missouri.

Wyatt sticks a blade of grass in his mouth and
rolls onto his back, looking up.

WYATT'S POV. Branches, leaves, blue sky,
white clouds, sunlight. A bird flies by.

WYATT (OS)
Sounds good.

INT. DINING ROOM, SUTHERLAND
HOUSE—NIGHT
Wyatt is having dinner with Urilla's family: her
mother, her father MR. SUTHERLAND, and
her brother ERWIN (25). Wyatt is as uncomfortable as he gets (not very) and Mr. Sutherland is struggling to play the stern, wise patriarch (a role that does not come easily to him). They all are eating in an extended silence right now. Finally—

MR. SUTHERLAND
When do you expect to begin your practice, Wyatt?

WYATT
It may be a while yet, sir.
(he smiles)
The Judge says he's never seen anybody
make slower progress.

At first, Wyatt is the only one who thinks this is
amusing, though when Erwin finally registers it
between heaping mouthfuls, he laughs out loud.

ERWIN
That's because the law's so damn boring.

Wyatt laughs, but Erwin's father gives his son a
disapproving look.

URILLA
(her brother doesn't bother her
much)
Erwin, not everyone has the aptitude to
be a blacksmith.

ERWIN
I bet I could teach Wyatt here, if he's
willing to work at it.

WYATT
I appreciate that, Erwin. But I've found a
job.

This is news to everyone, including Urilla.

WYATT
I thought I oughta be able to make a living while I continue my studies. Since I
want to buy some property.

MR. SUTHERLAND
(pleased)
You can't go wrong owning property. It
shows you've made a commitment to a
place.

WYATT
Yes, sir. That's what my father always says.

This last destroys any comfort Mr. Sutherland has taken from the news; he frowns.

> URILLA
> What is it, Wyatt? What job?

> WYATT
> With the city police. I'm to be a constable.
>   (he looks at Urilla)
> I figure a man who's about to propose marriage better have a livelihood.

This silences everyone for quite a spell. Mr. Sutherland isn't sure what response he should have. He looks at his wife and sees that she is crying happily.

> MR. SUTHERLAND
> Would you like us to excuse you, Esther?

> MRS. SUTHERLAND
> No, I'll stay right here.

She beams at Wyatt and Urilla through her tears.

> MR. SUTHERLAND
> When do you expect this proposal to happen, Wyatt, so we can all join in the crying?

> URILLA
> Daddy, Wyatt's proposed every day since he came back to town.

> MR. SUTHERLAND
>   (confused)
> Oh…

EXT. HOUSE FOR SALE, OUTSIDE OF LAMAR—DAY
POURING RAIN. There's a "FOR SALE" sign on the post of a little bungalow set on a pretty lot. Wyatt and Urilla have run from their buggy to the front porch and now Wyatt lets them in.

INT. FRONT ROOM/KITCHEN, HOUSE FOR SALE—DAY
Wyatt and Urilla, shaking off the rain, come into the tiny little house. It shows the signs of many previous tenants. They look around. Urilla goes in to inspect the kitchen. Wyatt stands in the threshold looking at her.

WYATT'S POV. Urilla's hair has gotten wet,

but she looks more beautiful than ever. Wyatt loves every inch of her and that is the view we're getting now. When she turns to him (and TO CAMERA) a special look crosses her face. She comes toward him.

As she passes close by him, he puts a hand on her arm. She looks up at him, then moves into the bedroom. He watches her a moment, then follows.

INT. BEDROOM, HOUSE FOR SALE—DAY
Urilla is standing at the window in the empty little room looking out at the rain. Wyatt comes in and stands next to her. He looks down on her. She is crying. He reaches up to touch a tear on her cheek. She turns to him with a kind of volcanic energy and puts her arms around him, kissing him passionately. It lasts a long time. When it's over, she steps back, flushed, gasping, no longer crying. She has her back against the wall and she looks at him hungrily, her eyes like burning coals. He moves up to her and she takes him violently in her arms.

Now we're seeing them from the front room, framed by the door to the bedroom.

EXT. HOUSE FOR SALE—DAY
The rain pours down. We TILT UP to the dark, roiling sky, thick with laden clouds. As we watch, the clouds miraculously BEGIN TO CLEAR as we—

DISSOLVE TO:
White, fluffy clouds, blue sky and sunshine. We TILT DOWN to—

EXT. HILLTOP, EDGE OF LAMAR—DAY
There is a magnificent tree at the top of the little hill. Under its generous branches, Wyatt Earp is marrying Urilla Sutherland. Judge Earp performs the ceremony and all the Earps are in attendance, just as Wyatt predicted.

This is the first time we see the adult Morgan (19). He's a handsome young rake, catnip to the girls, a fellow who knows how to enjoy himself. James (30) has settled into a life of affable, contented alcoholism; his face is dissipated. Virgil (27) looks much tougher, more weathered than last seen, though not yet the immovable oak of a man he is to become.

Vows are exchanged and the newlyweds kiss.

EXT. MEADOW AT BASE OF HILL—DAY
The wedding celebration continues at tables set up in the meadow. Wyatt walks through the party with Virgil.

WYATT
Will you be going back to Kansas?

VIRGIL
Not sure. A fellow used to ride shotgun with me went up to South Dakota to prospect. I might look him up, see what that's all about.

WYATT
(intrigued)
Prospecting? I have a mind to try that myself.

VIRGIL
You're a married man. You got responsibilities.

Virgil is looking at Urilla up ahead. Nicholas stands with his arm around her shoulder while Morgan talks to her.

WYATT
I got lucky.

VIRGIL

That's what Morgan thinks.

Wyatt and Virgil reach the others.

NICHOLAS

You got here just in time, Wyatt. Morgan is trying to convince your bride she's made a terrible mistake.

MORGAN

Picked the wrong brother.

URILLA

Morgan wants to know if there are any more at home like me.

WYATT

Did you tell him about Erwin?

Nicholas gives Urilla a squeeze, then releases her to Wyatt, who takes her in his arms. Nicholas is about to head off toward Virginia, who is nearby with the Earp grandparents.

NICHOLAS
(to Wyatt)

I wouldn't leave her alone too long, if I were you.

URILLA

Wyatt, I believe every man in your family is a terrible flirt.

VIRGIL
(taking her hand)

Except for me. I know how to treat a pretty young girl right.

Urilla and the other two brothers laugh.

EXT. THE LITTLE HOUSE—NIGHT

MOONLIGHT. Wyatt and Urilla move away from a wagon which has been festooned with flowers. They have been unwillingly escorted here by Morgan, Virgil, and two Local Girls, all of whom are tipsy. Morgan is shouting ribald encouragement to the newlyweds as Virgil gets their wagon rolling off into the night. Wyatt and Urilla wave them off, laughing.

Urilla has prepared the house for their arrival. Cheery curtains show in the windows. The couple is kissing as they walk up to the front door. At the threshold, Wyatt scoops her up dramatically and carries her inside. He kicks the front door shut behind them.

EXT. BEHIND THE LITTLE HOUSE—DAY

Wyatt and Urilla are working in the vegetable garden behind the house. It's hard, sweaty work and they're both concentrating on what they're doing. But there's contentment here. They talk as they work.

INT. BEDROOM, THE LITTLE HOUSE—NIGHT

SOMEONE'S POV of the window. A heavy snow is falling outside.

It's Urilla who is looking at it. She lies awake next to Wyatt, who sleeps beside her under a thick comforter. She is completely in repose, at peace. She looks at Wyatt's sleeping face. Then she begins to kiss him—eyebrows, eyes, mouth. As he sleepily comes to life, she moves over him. The comforter is so thick, you can barely discern her movement.

INT. BEDROOM, THE LITTLE HOUSE—SUNRISE

Wyatt is asleep next to Urilla, who is awake. She seems to be trying to hold herself very still, her hands on her belly, which has the first swell of pregnancy. It doesn't work. She leaps from the bed and runs from the room to be sick.

INT. FRONT ROOM, THE LITTLE HOUSE—NIGHT

Wyatt and Urilla are having dinner. Urilla has not touched the food on her plate. Wyatt studies her face. Now Urilla puts down the fork she has been holding and leans forward, putting her face in her hands.

WYATT
I thought this was only supposed to happen in the morning.

URILLA
Please, Wyatt, let's not talk about it!

She lifts her head and Wyatt is shocked by what he sees. Not only is she crying, but her face is covered in sweat.

WYATT
Urilla…

URILLA
Can't you let me be!

She stands abruptly from the table, wiping her eyes with her napkin. She has taken only two steps when she collapses on the floor.

EXT. THE LITTLE HOUSE—NIGHT

A Doctor's buggy is parked in front.

INT. BEDROOM, THE LITTLE HOUSE—NIGHT

DR. SEGER sits on the edge of the bed next to Urilla. Wyatt leans over her from the other side, mopping her brow with a cloth. Together they draw the blanket off Urilla's body. The doctor unbuttons her sweat-soaked top to reveal her swollen stomach. There are faint RED SPOTS on her skin. The doctor reacts. Wyatt looks at him in confusion.

EXT. FRONT PATH, THE LITTLE HOUSE—NIGHT

Mr. and Mrs. Sutherland are hurrying from their wagon toward the front door. Dr. Seger rushes out of the house and holds up a hand to stop them.

DR. SEGER
You can't go in.

MRS. SUTHERLAND
(coming ahead)
I want to see my girl!…

Dr. Seger actually grabs her and restrains her.

DR. SEGER
Esther, I can't allow it.

Mr. Sutherland, trying to remain calm, takes his wife under his control.

MR. SUTHERLAND
Has something gone wrong with the pregnancy?

DR. SEGER
(shakes his head)
This has nothing to do with that…It's typhoid.

The Sutherlands react in horror, seeming to shrink in size before our eyes.

DR. SEGER
I'm going to have to quarantine the house.

Mrs. Sutherland cries out and breaks away from her husband. Again she attempts to get past the doctor. Again he stops her forcefully.

DR. SEGER
I can't let you in, Esther! It's not fair to the town.

Mrs. Sutherland sinks down to the floor of the porch, sobbing.

EXT. SIDE OF THE LITTLE HOUSE—DAY
A beautiful Spring day. Lovely wildflowers have sprouted along the side of the house. The camera MOVES UP to the window of the bedroom. Wyatt sits at the side of Urilla's bed. He is tenderly administering a cold sponge bath to Urilla's nearly naked body.

INT. BEDROOM, THE LITTLE HOUSE—DAY
Urilla stirs, half-conscious. She takes a moment to focus on her surroundings. Her head turns and she sees Wyatt. He takes her hand. She squeezes it as hard as she can.

URILLA
(in terror)
…Oh, Wyatt…

Her face collapses and a horrible sound escapes from deep in her chest. Her grip on his hand relaxes. That's where Wyatt looks first, at their hands. Then quickly into her eyes. She is gone. Wyatt cannot accept it. He gathers her body into a fierce embrace.

EXT. THE LITTLE HOUSE—DAY
Out here, there is only the sound of BIRDS and the wind RUSTLING the leaves. The house

looks peaceful in its green setting. It's a beautiful day.

EXT. CEMETERY, LAMAR—DAY
Urilla Sutherland is laid to rest. Words are said. Wyatt stands a little apart from everyone else. As the others watch the coffin disappear into the ground, Wyatt abruptly turns and walks away from the grave without a backward glance. All alone.

EXT. THE LITTLE HOUSE—NIGHT
There is no light in the house and at first it appears there is no one here. Then we discern the dark shape of Wyatt, kneeling on the grass.

MOVING CLOSER ON WYATT. We see something we won't ever see again: He is crying. Now he looses a HORRIBLE SOUND toward the full moon. It is QUIET again. He lifts a bottle of whiskey to his mouth and drinks.

WIDE SHOT of the house, the yard, Wyatt's horse tied to a post by the road. Wyatt struggles to his feet and lurches toward the house. The rail in front stops his movement.

There is a flash of white handkerchief in the moonlight, then the spark of a match, then the flame of the burning handkerchief in the neck of the whiskey bottle. Wyatt raises his arm and heaves the burning bottle through the front window. Inside the house, it explodes. Wyatt backs drunkenly away.

AT HIS HORSE, Wyatt can barely get into the saddle. He looks off at the house, which is going up fast, then kicks his horse and rides off. Away from town. Away from life as he has known it. Down the road, into the darkness…

FADE TO BLACK.

FADE IN:
INT. STABLE, MADISON, ARKANSAS
(TWO MONTHS LATER)—NIGHT
A big, rough STABLE HAND leads a horse in from the street and back through the gloomy stable to a rear stall. As he tries to lead the horse into the stall, the mare WHINNIES and shies, afraid to enter. The Stable Hand looks in the stall: the hay in the corner is moving. There's a body in there. The Stable Hand grabs a pitchfork and moves into the stall to poke at the stirring body, which rolls over into the light.

It is Wyatt, though he is barely recognizable as the fresh-faced young man we've known thus far. He's been on a two-month, alcoholic bender. Some light has gone out of his eyes. He's lost his faith in the world. The Stable Hand lifts Wyatt roughly by the armpits and gives him the bum's rush down the center of the stable toward the street.

STABLE HAND
This ain't no hotel, ya stinkin' bum…I can't tell ya from the horse crap.

EXT. STREET—NIGHT
The Stable Hand sends Wyatt flying into the dirt of the street. A hitched horse nearby shies, but there are no humans in the vicinity to observe the event. Wyatt takes a while to pull himself together and get up. He's wearing the same outfit he was wearing the night he burned his house, but it is filthy.

The nearest saloon and a restaurant, where there is activity, are a half block away. A couple of Cowhands ride by and give Wyatt a glance before moving off. A TRAVELER rides down the street toward Wyatt and turns in across the way. Wyatt watches his progress, then walks across the street to where the man is hitching his horse. There is a croak in Wyatt's speech now.

WYATT
Pardon me, sir. I wonder if you could spare a fellow the price of a meal.

TRAVELER
You're drunk.

WYATT
No, sir, not at present.

TRAVELER
You reek of it…and worse. I'm not in the business of helping drunks.

The Traveler steps up on the sidewalk, moving away. Wyatt follows.

WYATT
You are correct, mister. I have done my share of drinking lately. But I intend to correct my behavior. And it would be a good start if you could lend me the price of a meal.

TRAVELER
There is no excuse for drunkenness. Or for the self-pity which so often occasions it.

Wyatt humbly acknowledges that, head bowed, but something ugly flashes through his eyes for an instant. The Traveler does not see it. He looks at Wyatt with distaste another moment.

TRAVELER
If you really want a meal, come with me and I'll arrange it. But I won't give you money.

WYATT
(eyes dead)
Thank you, sir. I accept.

Wyatt comes up onto the sidewalk next to the man, who reacts to Wyatt's smell. They start off toward the lights of the saloon. Wyatt looks around.

TRAVELER
Please, don't walk so close…
(Wyatt drops back a step)
I don't know if they'll serve you here, but maybe they'll let you eat out back—

They have reached the mouth of a dark alley. Wyatt suddenly grabs the Traveler forcefully around the neck and half-drags, half-throws him into the shadows.

EXT. ALLEY —NIGHT
The Traveler is slammed up against the wall, his head banging. Wyatt hits him in the face and the stomach; the man crumples to the ground GROANING. Wyatt quickly goes through his pockets (he's done this before) and extracts the man's money belt. He takes the cash and drops the money belt on the Traveler. Wyatt picks up the man's hat and tries it on; it almost fits.

WYATT
(poisonous, to the Traveler)
You don't know what you're talking about!

Wyatt hurries away, looking around.

EXT. STREET—NIGHT
Wyatt comes back down the sidewalk to the Traveler's horse. Wyatt thinks about it for a split second, then unhitches the horse, swings up and wheels the horse out. He rides out of town at a gallop.

EXT. LIVERY, PINE BLUFF, ARKANSAS— DAY
Wyatt sells the Traveler's horse to the Owner of the livery. He counts his cash and pockets it as he ambles off toward town.

INT. BROTHEL, PINE BLUFF, ARKANSAS —NIGHT
Wyatt soaks in a wooden bath tub in this bro-ken-down whorehouse. He takes a long pull from a whiskey bottle. A fat, pock-marked

whore named PARIS settles on a stool by the tub and regards Wyatt with some curiosity.

PARIS
That's a little better. Leastwise I can take you in my bed without foulin' it.

WYATT
I'm sure you have your standards.

PARIS
Don't think I don't.
(a long look)
You're pretty new at this, ain't you?

WYATT
At what?

PARIS
At makin' a wreck of yerself.

WYATT
(laughs without humor)
It won't last much longer.

PARIS
(heard it before)
Gonna reform, are you, Ace?

WYATT
(shakes his head "no")
Reckon to get myself shot dead pretty
soon.

Paris was not prepared for that answer. She lifts
a shabby towel.

PARIS
Let's find out what's left of you…

As Wyatt begins to rise, the door behind him
bursts open and the large Sheriff of Pine Bluff
bursts in, gun in hand. He smashes Wyatt over
the head with it. Wyatt sinks down in the dirty
water, turning it purple. Several whore and johns
are peering in from the hallway. Pushing through
them comes the Livery Owner who bought the
horse from Wyatt.

"YOU'RE PRETTY NEW AT THIS, AIN'T YOU?" "AT WHAT?" "AT MAKIN' A WRECK OF YERSELF."

Wyatt had some pretty normal things happen to him. Tragic they were, but they were fairly normal. Women died in childbirth. People died of typhoid. It happened back then. He wasn't the first man to have that happen. He behaved as any one of us might have—he really grieved. He was truly in love and that was taken away from him. That sent him on a spiral that a lot of men in this world have had to endure and experience. And he almost didn't come out of it. He really had to look himself in the mirror and get hold of himself before he was completely lost. It's like a drunk who makes it out just in time, finds AA or something that snaps him out of it.

"Also, it was very unusual for a man of this time to just stop drinking, altogether. So that spiraling period must have been pretty miserable."
—KEVIN COSTNER

Wyatt actually did have a period of dissipation. He was arrested for stealing a horse, and did, in fact, run out on an indictment. He was a fugitive. He was clearly in a bad place in his life, and willing to do anything, he had that kind of recklessness. It was a moment at which he could have become an outlaw, as a lot of these lawmen were previously outlaws or became outlaws after they were lawmen."
—LAWRENCE KASDAN

INT. JAIL CELL, PINE BLUFF,
ARKANSAS—NIGHT
Outside the small cell window: driving rain,
lightning, THUNDER.

A tubercular Inmate is coughing horribly. It
goes on and on. Finally, he crawls on his hands
and knees to the corner of the cell, where he
loudly coughs up some of his insides. Not far
from the resting head of—

Wyatt, who doesn't even react. He's gotten used
to such things. He just stares at the ceiling,
halfway to oblivion. A cockroach crawls across
his chest and disappears down the side of his
neck. No reaction.

CLOSE ON WYATT'S EYES. He's somewhere
else.

WHAT WYATT SEES: Urilla working in the
sunny garden of the little house, as though seen
from WYATT'S POV. This FADES and he sees—
Urilla at the moment of her death, sweaty,
gaunt and wasted, speaking her last words,
WYATT'S POV. This FADES and he sees—

The view in front of the wagon train at night in
the Mojave Desert, WYATT'S POV moving
toward dark mountains in the distance. It now
appears to be the region of Death. This FADES
and he sees—

Wyatt's father, Nicholas Earp, behind jail bars.

Wyatt stares, horrified. It takes him a moment
to realize that this image is not in his mind. We
are back in the jail cell. Nicholas has in fact
been admitted to the jailblock and stands staring down at his prodigal son, caught somewhere
between contempt and compassion. Rainwater
drips from his hat and coat. He looks twice as
formidable as we've ever seen him, like a biblical Elder, and we understand how this line of
tough men sprang from his loins.

WYATT (OS)
Pa.

Nicholas extends a dripping sleeve through the
bars; his long, crooked fingers beckon, like those
of the Grim Reaper, for Wyatt to come to him.
When Wyatt moves closer, Nicholas grabs him
ferociously by his shirt and pulls him up to face
him through the bars.

NICHOLAS
Horse thief!

Wyatt looks with shame into his eyes, then acknowledges it.

WYATT
How did you find—

NICHOLAS
Shut up!
          (the older man tightens his grip)
Do you want to die? That's what we do to horse thieves, we hang them.

WYATT
I don't care.

If anything, the father's look gets harder.

NICHOLAS
Do you think you're the first man to lose someone? That's what this life is all about…loss. We don't use it as an excuse to destroy ourselves. We go on. All of us. Even you. Because you're…

Nicholas relaxes his grip for the first time, but Wyatt stays where he is.

NICHOLAS
…because you're an Earp.

Wyatt receives this, deeply. It may be the first thing he's accepted in a long time.

NICHOLAS
You're getting out of here.

EXT. PINE BLUFF—NIGHT
A THUNDERSTORM. Wyatt and Nicholas are shielded by an overhang from the driving rain. There is a saddled horse tied nearby, nervous in the storm.

NICHOLAS
I paid them $500 bail. I told them I'd defend you at your trial. But there's not going to be a trial.

Wyatt is shocked to hear this from his father.

NICHOLAS
If they try you, they'll hang you. If they catch you, they'll hang you.

Nicholas suddenly enfolds Wyatt in his arms.

NICHOLAS
So you get on that horse and ride. And you keep on riding until you're out of Arkansas…and you don't come back here, ever.

Wyatt's face is on his father's shoulder. His shame for bringing the older man to this place on this night will stay with him forever. And cleanse a wound. Nicholas holds him tight for a moment, then pushes him on his way.

Wyatt moves out into the rain and mounts up. One last look at the older man, then he wheels the horse and gallops off into the storm. When he is at a distance, a FLASH OF LIGHTNING illuminates the world for an instant and, when it's over, we—

FADE TO BLACK.

"A MOVIE LIKE THIS IS REALLY HARD."

W hen I first read the script of *Wyatt Earp*, which might be maybe nine months ago now, ten months ago, it was a hundred and fifty some-odd pages and a very, very dense script, and it was a tremendous read. At the same time, as a producer, you're reading not only for story and character and how involved you get, but you're looking at it scene by scene to say, 'How can we possibly attempt to put all this on the screen? What's it gonna take?' And as I read, I kept a small calculation on the side, thinking, 'Well, this is gonna be thousands of extras,' which it ended up being. 'We're gonna have to shoot all over the country,' because it calls for Wyoming and Dodge and Wichita and Tombstone and on and on, and I thought, 'My God, we're gonna travel the country.' But it's ended up that we're centered here in Santa Fe, and we're shooting ninety-nine percent of the picture here in New Mexico—an hour and a half here, an hour and a half there, and it ends up, I think, being twenty-eight perfectly separate locations.

"In terms of scope, this will look very large, because, in truth, it is. There are over a hundred speaking roles, and I mean those people honestly have lines. In terms of size of towns, we've re-created Tombstone here and it's four square blocks. I don't know how many millions of board feet. It's now the largest Western town set in the world. So *Wyatt Earp*, in every regard—from extras to locations to cities we've built—is larger than anything I've been a part of.

"I think when you do a film of this size and this scope, it's important to keep a tone and keep an energy going, because we're shooting for nineteen weeks out here, and the elements get to you. It's sunny, and we'll go from July through mid-December. We go from the heat of the summer to the cold of the winter, and when you have a crew that is three to four hundred strong, and you count extras and construction and all that, there's just a general feel to a company, a momentum that gets started.

You get into a roll in maybe the second or third week. But to retain that for nineteen weeks is one of the most difficult things. And I see movies that have lost it, very clearly. Being a producer, you watch day in and day out that there's an energy that is provided and sustained for that period of time.

"There is a personality to a movie that can go awry. And I think the biggest challenge is that everybody remains intact and this family that you've built continues to not only survive, but get better, get stronger. And you feel that. There's a love that you put into your movies, and I think an audience reads that off the screen before anything. I know when a film has been loved and been taken care of for twenty weeks, as opposed to something that's been shoddily put together, where there was conflict, and we don't allow that on the set. It makes a big difference."

—JIM WILSON, PRODUCER

A movie like this is really hard. There's just so many people and so many things to coordinate. We sent our costume designer to Europe to find costumes. There weren't enough costumes in this country for a movie this size! There's so much money at stake that every little decision has to be thought through very carefully. And when you're outdoors so much, it's really hard. If it rains what do you do? You sit there and wait for it to stop raining, or you shoot in the rain. On *Silverado*, we lost about ten days waiting for the jet contrails to clear out of the sky [the smoke trails left by jets are, for obvious reasons, unacceptable in a supposedly nineteenth century sky.] Westerns are just very difficult.

"I've always said, 'Horses are hard. Trains are harder. And boats are the hardest.' This movie's got all three."

—CHARLES OKUN, EXECUTIVE PRODUCER
AND UNIT PRODUCTION MANAGER

C harlie's a great believer, as I am, in the idea that preparation is everything. If you prep a show properly, you have a very good chance of it

running well. If you don't prep it properly, you're behind right from the beginning. At least on higher budget films, there isn't a guy on the crew that doesn't have a lot of experience. They've all been around and done a lot of work. Maybe they've never done a Western on this scale, but they know how to make movies. Where you run into problems with some of these guys is if you don't give them information. Information becomes everything. Like if we didn't tell people how many extras there were in town, things like that—Well how many horses do you have? Twenty-five horses? Do you have a hundred horses? Do you have fifty saddles, a hundred saddles? How many people do you need? How many tables in the saloon? How many chairs? How many costumes? How many buses to get everyone there? How many lunches do we have to serve on the set? So it really comes down to asking Larry questions and everything that he answers has an effect on most all the departments. They're all touched by it. Whether it's a camera car, a crane, an extra electrician, extra cable, lights—you just need to make sure everything is covered. It all really revolves around Larry, and everything that he wants. There's a direct correlation between money and art, and you can't say yes to everything. Some of the things that we want to do become very expensive and they become a choice. A street looks more crowded with two hundred people on it than with one hundred, but it costs about twice as much. And if you can save money there, you can use it somewhere else."

—MICHAEL GRILLO, EXECUTIVE PRODUCER
AND UNIT PRODUCTION MANAGER

T his is the most complicated movie I've ever been on, but I don't like to think of it that way. I said before we started shooting that I didn't want to think of this as a big movie. I said it was like two little movies. Now I take that back. It's like three little movies."

—STEVE DUNN, FIRST ASSISTANT DIRECTOR

"I'm Wyatt Earp.
It all ends now!"

FADE IN:
EXT. GRASSLANDS, KANSAS (1871)—DAY
Lovely rolling plains, gentle slopes and valleys. The grass waves sleepily in the sunlight.

LOW ANGLE looking up at the crest of a rise. A SOUND GROWS slowly, a deep RUMBLE, the earth itself begins to tremble. Suddenly, coming right at us over the rise, here they are— a huge herd of BUFFALO, stampeding at a dead run.

ANOTHER ANGLE and we're looking across the backs of the enormous brown mass, like some dark plain come to life. It seems endless.

ON A HILL NEARBY, Wyatt is watching. He looks much better, but his experiences of the recent past have left an unmistakable mark upon him. There is a new hardness here, and lines in his face we have never seen. He's sitting on the seat of a wagon drawn by two horses, the back of which is heaped high with buffalo hides, the impressive product of his solitary labors.

As the center of the herd passes his position, he continues on his way, in the other direction.

EXT. HIDE LOT, BUFFALO CAMP, KANSAS PLAINS—DAY
This rough temporary community of tents and ramshackle buildings is only destined to last as long as buffalo remain in the vicinity. The hide lot at its center is filled with stack upon stack of buffalo hides waiting to be sent back East for processing. The place is abuzz with Hunters and their crews come to town to cash in their take.

Nearby, two young men in their early 20s, BAT MASTERSON and ED MASTERSON, are watching the arriving hunters with intensity, murmuring to each other. Now they see something that interests them a lot.

Wyatt is driving up to the hide lot with his full wagon, all alone.

INT. TENT SALOON—DAY
The place is half full. Wyatt is at the bar talking to the BARTENDER as Bat and Ed move up next to him.

        WYATT
How 'bout some hot coffee?

BARTENDER
We sell warm whiskey, not hot coffee.

Wyatt smacks a coin on the bar.

WYATT
Why don't you brew up some coffee?

BARTENDER
Coffee she is.

The Bartender takes the coin and moves off.

BAT
'Scuse me, mister…We saw you come in with your wagon. But we didn't see any skinners with you.

WYATT
That's 'cause there wasn't any.

BAT
Quit?

WYATT
Dead.

ED
Well that's as good as quit in my book. My brother and me are lookin' for work as skinners.

A huge bear of a man, a buffalo hunter named LINK, comes in and makes his way to the bar a few feet from Wyatt.

LINK
Bartender! My luck finally turned with those big stinkin' bastards. Whiskey all around!

The saloon denizens receive the news favorably as the Bartender begins to fill a row of glasses. Link focuses on Wyatt and slaps him on the back. The Bartender places a glass in front of Wyatt, who places his hand over it.

WYATT
No thanks.

The Bartender starts to move on, but Link stops him, turns on Wyatt.

LINK
Wait a second. Mister, Link Borland is buyin', so drink up.

WYATT
Thanks, but I got some coffee comin'. I don't do well on whiskey.

Wyatt meets Ed and Bat Masterson (Bill Pullman and Tom Sizemore, right).

LINK

I don't give a pail of hot spit what you do well on. If I'm buyin', you're drinkin'.

WYATT

Fair enough…if you'd pay for my coffee, I'd be much obliged.

Link grabs the whiskey bottle from the Bartender's hands and slams it down in front of Wyatt.

LINK

Drink!

Something clicks through Wyatt's eyes, something harder than we've seen. He looks at his hands, both of which are still on the bar.

WYATT

Mister, I been in a real bad mood for a couple of years…so why don't you leave me alone.

Link's hand drops to his gun. Suddenly, Wyatt's gun is in Link's face, cocked. It was too fast to follow. He is very calm.

WYATT

Drop your gunbelt and go away.

Link struggles to keep control of his functions. He unbuckles his holster and drops it to the floor, then backs away from Wyatt and out of

the saloon. Wyatt's eyes flick over the other customers. He uncocks his gun and holsters it. He turns back to the Mastersons, who regard him in stunned awe.

WYATT

You got any experience?

Ed and Bat exchange a quick glance. Wyatt looks them over.

BAT

A little.

WYATT

You know it ain't too hard shootin' a bunch of dumb animals…
        (he stops and faces them)
…skinning's the ugly part.

ED

Our mother didn't raise no shirkers.

WYATT

Twenty-five dollars a piece.

BAT

Huh?

WYATT

You want to be skinners. That's what I'll pay.

ED
Mister that's a deal. My name's Ed Masterson.
(shakes Wyatt's hand)
This is my brother…

BAT
(shaking hands)
…Bat.

WYATT
What?

BAT
Bat…Bat Masterson.

WYATT
(never heard that before)
Bat…okay, Bat…Wyatt Earp.

EXT. SLIGHT RISE, HUNTING GROUND—DAY
All we see at first is two sticks, crossed and tied in an X and planted firmly in the ground. Now the barrel of Wyatt's Sharp's "50" hunting rifle lowers carefully into the top V. Wyatt lies prone on the ground. Far behind him in a dip, Bat and Ed are crouched down, tending the three horses which brought them out here.

A herd of buffalo is grazing quietly on the flat plain beneath this rise, the closest not more than 50 yards away. Wyatt lines up a big bull in his sights, takes a deep breath and fires. The bull goes down. The other buffalo do not react.

WYATT'S FACE. He commences repeated firing. We STAY CLOSE on his face, seen through the smoke of his shotgun.

EXT. FLAT PLAIN BENEATH RISE—DAY
OVERHEAD SHOT. LATER. The herd is moving slowly out of frame, and now we see why: Wyatt is approaching on foot, gently waving his coat in the air and SHOUTING. As the herd moves away, they leave behind the casualties—twenty lifeless hulks dot the area.

LATER. GROUND LEVEL. Wyatt, Bat and Ed proceed with the grisly business of skinning a bull. Wyatt is on his horse 20 feet from the carcass. A line of rope is tied to the saddle horn and stretched taut to the body of the buffalo, where Bat has attached it to the bunched, heavy neck hide (it has been slit away from the head). Ed stands nearby, huge bloody skinning knife in his hand. As Wyatt urges his horse forward, the thick skin of the bull is pulled away from its body, revealing the bloody musculature.

Ed watches with growing revulsion, then can't take it anymore and turns away quickly to be sick in the grass.

EXT. THEIR CAMP, GRASSLANDS — MAGIC HOUR
A half dozen skins have been staked out for drying on the ground. Ed and Bat are pounding

another into place as Wyatt makes a campfire near their wagon.

EXT. CAMPFIRE—NIGHT
The remains of a buffalo roast is on the spit, but the three have had their fill.

> ED
> We got a brother named Jim, too.

> WYATT
> One brother? That's all you got, one measly brother?
> (Ed is offended, Bat laughs)
> Better than nothing, I guess.

Wyatt gets up and stokes the fire, looking into the flame—

> WYATT
> There's nothing counts so much as blood. Everybody else is just a stranger.

Ed and Bat exchange a look.

> BAT
> (to Ed)
> I guess we know where we stand with Wyatt here.

> WYATT
> (laughs)
> You boys keep up that good skinnin', you just might get to be family yet. 'Course, before you can be family I'd have to know where you got that name "Bat."

Ed laughs. He watches Bat become suddenly squirmy.

> BAT
> It's just my name, I already told you ten times. They always called me that.

Now Ed rolls over in a laughing fit.

> BAT
> Shut up, Ed!

> WYATT
> I'll tell you what, Ed. You tell me his real name and I'll let you do some of the shootin' tomorrow.

> ED
> (instantly)
> It's Bartholomew! Bartholomew Masterson!

Bat throws his coffee cup at Ed's head; he ducks it neatly, laughing.

> WYATT
> Bartholomew?
> (turns to Bat, fighting a grin)
> Why, Bat, that's a beautiful name. No reason to be ashamed of a twenty-five-dollar handle like that. Maybe I'll just call you that all the time…Bartholomew.

EXT. HIDE LOT, BUFFALO CAMP, KANSAS PLAINS—DAY
The place is abuzz with Hunters and their crews come to town to cash in their take. Three Indians, wearing western clothing, ride by. They cast a mournful gaze at the evidence of the mass slaughter that has devastated their way of life.

Wyatt, Bat and Ed are at a barrel. Wyatt has divided a thick stack of cash into three equal piles. He takes his own. Ed and Bat exchange looks.

> ED
> We said we'd work for you. The Mastersons are as good as their word…we'll stick to the bargain.

> WYATT
> I tell you, so much has happened, I can't rightly remember what bargain we made.

> BAT
> Wyatt—

The men exchange a quiet look, which embarrasses Wyatt. A deep bond has been formed here. They shake hands.

> ED
> Thanks, Wyatt.

> BAT
> We got room in our family for another brother if you ever find the need.

> WYATT
> Come on, let's get us a good buffalo steak.

Ed gives him a disgusted look, then all three laugh and start down the road toward town.

> ED
> Sure you won't change your mind and take one more run at 'em?

43

OWEN ROIZMAN, CINEMATOGRAPHER

Before we started, I didn't have any really set visual plan for the picture—it sort of evolved. But I had certain ideas. I've tried to capture what I felt it might have looked like in those days—dark interiors and warm color interiors, bright, hot daylight, a lot of dust, mud, smoke, all those elements. I tried to incorporate all those things into every shot, whenever possible.

"Larry and I both love the wide-screen format, we've used it on several films. It gives the picture a bigger feeling. In this particular instance, it adds tremendous dimension because you can get so much into the frame. As far as lens choice, we've

tried to make *Wyatt Earp* big in feeling by not getting too tight for our closeups, trying to get as many wide shots as we can. We've only used long lenses sparingly, so that we always feel the scope of the picture.

"That was basically my design—to keep the interiors and nights dark, the days bright, to keep the shots wide and to try and get as many shots of the sunset and things like that as possible.

"Larry and I like the same kinds of things. It's a wonderful association. We like to joke with one another and be serious at the same time. I have great respect for him and I think he has the same

for me. Some directors have really strong opinions about every light, every composition. Others just leave you alone completely because they don't know anything about [photography]; they're only concerned with the actors. Larry's the best combination of the two. He's involved and he has opinions, but he lets me do my thing."
　　　　　　　—OWEN ROIZMAN

The director and the director of photography are both struggling to make the look of the film appropriate to the material. A good DP will always be able to do that. You're trying to find someone with enormous skills—lighting skills

and composition you relate to. And then, maybe most important, you have to have a relationship that works for you. I always say that the most important collaboration, during production, is with the cinematographer. So you're looking for that relationship to be one of open communication, with a respectful hearing of each other's ideas, and, hopefully, some sort of collaboration that's productive for everybody.

"Owen's been doing beautiful work for twenty-five years, in many different genres. He's shot several movies that I love—*The French Connection, The Exorcist, Three Days of the Condor,* and about ten other movies that influenced the way I think about how movies should look. And I have a great time with him, while doing this very exhausting work. A good relationship between a director and a cinematographer is a lot like a good marriage, in that the longer it lasts and the closer the relationship becomes, less needs to be discussed in order to reach the end you're looking for." —LAWRENCE KASDAN

CAROL LITTLETON, EDITOR

My relationship with Larry has probably been the most important of my professional career. I think that there was a kindred spirit that I could detect, even in reading the script, before working together, on *Body Heat* [*Kasdan's first film, and the first of six collaborations between Littleton and Kasdan*]. There was a tremendous respect for the genre, a sense of having something important to say, and being able to do it with a keen eye to detail. He also has a wonderful ear for the characters' voices, along with a sense of humor for the most mundane situations. Being able to extract the essence of human discourse…. *Body Heat* had that connection, and every script that Larry writes has that. There is a thread throughout Larry's work that is very consistent. There's a tremendous humanity, an enjoyment in watching people, how they walk through life, literally where they place their feet, and a keen observation of the detail that can be managed in such a way that it is dramatic." —CAROL LITTLETON

I think we share an interest in the same subjects of human life. Carol approaches editing entirely through the thematic material, and from that, the narrative. She doesn't approach it in terms of montage. That's not her first thought, in terms of cutting two pieces of film together. She always starts with the material. And the material that I have chosen to work on is very much in line with her sensibility and interests. We made that connection very early on. She was able to relate to the stuff that I wanted to do very strongly and passionately. It happens that she's also a great editor. That's what you're looking for, that combination of shared interests and passions, and great facility, skills, and talent. You can have an interesting intellectual conversation with a friend, but they can't cut your movie. You can have an interesting intellectual conversation with Carol about the material and she can cut your movie."

—LAWRENCE KASDAN

WYATT
Nah. I'm going to visit my brother James over in Wichita, meet his wife, and see if I can figure some better way to make a livin' than—

ED
—shootin' a bunch of dumb animals.

Wyatt nods. He remembers saying that. But there is some added gravity in his look now as he recalls the experiences on the plains.

BAT
Don't seem to hold much future, that's for sure— not with every asshole in the territory pluggin' away dawn 'til dusk.

The three friends consider that a moment. They're some of the assholes. They begin to laugh.

INT. PRYOR'S SALOON, WICHITA (1874)—NIGHT
FULL SCREEN, the playing surface of a Faro bank. We hear Wyatt's Voice calling out the bets.

David Andrews as James Earp

Wyatt, dressed much more civilized now (clean-shaven, still no mustache), is behind the table, running the game with some skill and assurance. He's so proficient, in fact, that he can occasionally look up across the crowded barroom to catch a look at —

His brother James tending bar, along with a couple other Bartenders, behind the endless expanse of dark wood. Right now, James is leaning over the end of the bar to talk confidentially with a whore named BESSIE. She has her hand on his, and as the conversation ends, she gives his cheek a rough, affectionate pat, then moves back into the hubbub of carousing Cowboys, Gamblers and Railroad Men.

An OLDER DEALER moves in to take Wyatt's place. Wyatt moves out and crosses to James' area of the bar. James sees him and brings over a pot of coffee, from which he pours Wyatt a cup.

JAMES
How's it going?

WYATT
I'm getting the hang of it. I like that game. I wouldn't mind owning a place, I tell you that.

JAMES
(laughs)
Last week you wanted us to start a stage line…or was that the silver mine? Now we're gonna have our own saloon.

WYATT
Why not? You know how to run a place. If we got Morg and Virgil over here and put all our savings together…I know there's not much future in working for other people.

JAMES
I wouldn't count on Morg puttin' too much away. His specialty is throwin' it away…

James is looking at the stairs at the back of the room. Bessie is leading a Cowboy to the brothel upstairs as another Whore and Customer come down.

JAMES
(considering)
Who knows…with what Bessie makes, maybe we could get a bit together.
(catches Wyatt's look)
She's my wife, Wyatt.

WYATT
You know I don't like counting on women.

JAMES
Hell, I'd count on Bessie ahead of any man I know. What do ya got against her, anyhow?

WYATT
(hard for him)
Well…she's a whore, James.

JAMES
Yes she is, Wyatt…and a hard-working one at that.

WYATT
What are you doin' with her?

JAMES
The same thing everyone else is doin' with her, Wyatt. The only difference is she doesn't charge me.

WYATT
And it doesn't bother you?

JAMES
That she doesn't charge me? Why no, I'm rather fond of the arrangement. On a good day I can even get her to cook and clean a little.

Wyatt looks away, giving up.

JAMES
What was that? I didn't hear you.

WYATT
Nothin'…if your arrangement doesn't bother you, I guess it doesn't bother me.

JAMES
That's a big load off my mind, Wyatt. I been losin' sleep worryin' about whether or not my arrangement bothered you.

A Customer down the bar calls for James and he moves away. Wyatt watches him go. Then he considers the room and its denizens. It's a long way from Urilla and Lamar, Missouri. There's a kind of resignation in his look. Maybe this harsher world is where he was meant to spend his days.

JoBeth Williams as Bessie Earp, on stairs.

47

INT. WYATT'S ROOM, BOARDING HOUSE—DAY

Wyatt is just getting up. Still barefoot, he's wearing pants and a long underwear top. After rinsing his face in a washbowl on the dresser, he lifts his head to look in the dirty mirror.

A bullet SHATTERS the front window of the room. Wyatt doesn't react much. He looks out the window with annoyance. There is more GUNFIRE out there, but it isn't aimed up here. There are the SOUNDS of YELLING and RUNNING ABOUT. Then a few more shots.

WYATT
What the hell…?

He goes out the door.

EXT. MAIN STREET, WICHITA—DAY

Wyatt comes out onto the wooden sidewalk in front of the boarding house. There is a group of men gathered in the alley next door. Others can be seen cowering behind posts and horse troughs. They're all looking at the Iron Spike Saloon across the way. There are two more GUNSHOTS inside the saloon and the front window of the saloon SHATTERS. One of the bullets hits the wall near Wyatt as he makes his way to the alley. He reacts and moves down among the men, where a vigorous discussion is going on between MAYOR WILSON and DEPUTY FORD.

MAYOR WILSON
Where's Marshal Meagher?

DEPUTY FORD
He's in Kansas City.

MAYOR WILSON
Kansas City? What in tarnation…Okay, Ford, you're going to have to go in there.

DEPUTY FORD
The hell I will. That's Rowdy Dubbs.

WYATT
What's going on, Mayor?

MAYOR WILSON
Rowdy Dubbs is in the Iron Spike drunk and mad. We think he's already shot one man. Ford here's got to go in and get him.

Ford shakes his head, looking at the saloon.

WYATT
(to Ford)
That's your job, isn't it?

Ford takes the badge off his chest and hands it to the Mayor.

DEPUTY FORD
Not anymore…they don't pay me enough to commit suicide.

More GUNFIRE. People down the street react to a near-miss. Wyatt looks over at the saloon.

WYATT
Hell…what's his name?

MAYOR WILSON
Rowdy Dubbs.

WYATT
Never heard of him…
(extends an open hand for Ford's revolver)
Gimme.

Ford hands over his six-gun. Wyatt checks the cylinder, weighs it in his hand, then spins it once, with a lovely expertise. Wyatt runs across the street toward the saloon. There are more GUNSHOTS and the sound of GLASS SHATTERING inside the saloon.

Wyatt reaches the front wall of the saloon, ducks low under the window and moves gracefully to the side of the swinging doors. He straightens up and waits a moment, totally still, listening. There is one more GUNSHOT and another window blasts out.

Wyatt dives suddenly through the swinging doors, disappearing down onto the floor of the saloon. There are TWO SHOTS, and then silence. Then MOANING. We hear FOOTSTEPS, more MOANING.

WYATT (OS)
Shut up, fellow.

There is the unmistakable sound of someone being hit over the head. The MOANING stops. We hear a body being DRAGGED. Wyatt comes out the swinging doors dragging the unconscious Rowdy Dubbs by his right foot. His left thigh is bleeding from a bullet wound. Wyatt drags him down a step and deposits him in the

middle of the dusty street. The crowd converges on him.

> WYATT
> I don't see anybody else in there, but maybe you better check around.

> MAYOR WILSON
> Young man, how would you like a job?

> WYATT
> I got a job over at Pryor's dealing Faro.

> MAYOR WILSON
> Seventy-five dollars a month.

This gives Wyatt pause, it's a big hike. He considers.

> WYATT
> I don't know… being a deputy isn't exactly—

> MAYOR WILSON
> I'll make it one hundred, but don't try to hold me up for more.

> WYATT
> A hundred dollars a month…?

The Mayor pins the badge on Wyatt's underwear top. Wyatt does not stop him.

> WYATT
> What's the Marshal gonna say?

> MAYOR WILSON
> Oh, Marshal Meagher's going to like you just fine…deputy.

The crowd begins to disperse, taking Rowdy Dubbs roughly along with them. Wyatt, in a bit of a daze, soon stands alone in the center of the street. There is a Colt .45 in his hand and a badge on his chest. He looks down at it.

He's a Lawman.

EXT. DEAD LINE, MAIN STREET, WICHITA—NIGHT
ANGLE ON the "Dead Line" Sign. It reads: "WICHITA DEAD LINE—Wearing of Firearms beyond this Point is *strictly prohibited* by Law."

Wyatt is beyond the sign, walking into the heart of the raucous Wichita Sporting District, at the side of MARSHAL MIKE MEAGHER, a big man in his forties. The street is hopping with all kinds of men out for a good time, plus a healthy assortment of women who will give it to them. The many saloons are buzzing.

MEAGHER
…they're not bad boys, most of 'em. Just been on the trail a long time. Now their pockets are full of cash, they're thirsty and horny. You can understand that, can't you?

WYATT
Yes sir.

MEAGHER
Real polite. I like that. I figure if I can just separate the drinkin' from the firearms, our establishments will be able to separate the cowboy from his money without any harm comin' to anyone.

Wyatt takes this all in as his eyes scan the street. He and Meagher both see a couple of Cowboys approaching, one of whom is wearing a gun.

MEAGHER
'Course the problem arises when a fellow crosses the Dead Line with his weapon in tow.

MEAGHER (cont'd)
(Meagher indicates the Cowboys to Wyatt)
What do we do then?

WYATT
We disarm them.

MEAGHER
Nope.

They're closing the distance to the two Cowboys. With sudden quickness, Meagher draws his gun from its holster and brutally WHACKS the armed Cowboy over the head. It's pretty shocking. The Cowboy goes down hard in the dirt. Wyatt covers the other Cowboy as Meagher bends and removes the first Cowboy's gun from the prone body.

MEAGHER
(to Wyatt)
The theory here bein' that an unconscious cowboy is much less likely to shoot you. You may then inform the cowboy that he is under arrest.

Meagher looks down at the unconscious Cowboy.

MEAGHER
You're under arrest.

Meagher looks over at the Cowboy's friend.

MEAGHER
You can pick him and his gun up at my jail in the morning.

The second Cowboy nods, frowning, and hurries away. Meagher looks at Wyatt.

MEAGHER
Does that seem a little harsh to you?

WYATT
("no")
Not so harsh as seeing him shoot somebody.

INT. CITY JAIL—NIGHT
Wyatt, Meagher and a huge Ferocious Teamster burst into the cellblock. The Ferocious Teamster is bleeding from the head—the blood has covered his whole face—but he is unbowed. It takes all of the two lawmen's strength to slam him into a cell, where the other Prisoners scurry to give him a wide berth. The Ferocious Teamster rushes back at Wyatt, who's standing at the front bars of the cell. Wyatt's fist meets his face as he arrives. He goes down hard.

Wyatt and Meagher look down at the Ferocious Teamster, then up at each other. Meagher gives Wyatt an impressed and approving nod. They both begin to laugh.

EXT. IRON SPIKE SALOON—NIGHT
Wyatt and Meagher come out of the busy saloon, making their rounds. The windows of the saloon are boarded up where Rowdy Dubbs shot them out. They look around. Meagher looks out at the street and sees something that concerns him. Wyatt follows his look.

MEAGHER
This could be trouble.

Wyatt smiles. Indeed the fellow crossing the street looks as if he could be trouble. He wears two guns and looks as if he knows how to use them. But, as he ambles toward them grinning, we recognize him.

WYATT
Don't shoot him, Mike. This is my no-good brother Morgan.

MORGAN
How are ya, Wyatt?

MEAGHER
As opposed to your no-good brother James?

STUNT COORDINATOR NORMAN HOWELL

WHAT IT MEANS TO BE STUNT COORDINATOR ON WYATT EARP
Before we even started production [Larry Kasdan and I] sat down and had a meeting about each and every stunt—how to make it as real as possible, but still be safe. Larry is very safety conscious which makes it very easy. If something doesn't look quite right to either of us, we work it out to make it completely safe. We talked about where we were going to use cable jerks, if we wanted to see a certain squib [or gunshot hit], where's it's going to happen.

"A lot of the actors that are working with horses have never ridden before, so there's a lot that goes on behind the scenes that you don't really know about.

A lot of people think of a stunt as a guy falling off a building, but anything that becomes physical is stunt work. Whether it's riding a horse or taking a bullet hit."

THE REALISTIC NATURE OF THE STUNTS IN WYATT EARP
I think it's better if the audience can relate to [a stunt] as being realistic, I think you grab them a lot more than you do if it's over the top, they don't feel it as much. An unusual thing on this show is that the actors are doing all their own stunts. I don't know, in my career, of any show that's used actors to do their own stunts as often as we have on this. And they're all doing a great job. They're all really gung-ho about it,

which really makes it work. They put in the time to learn to do it right."

THE CHANGING WORLD OF STUNTS
There are some veterans, that have been doing it a long time, they come in and they do things the way they've always been doing them. There's nothing wrong with that, but it's a little more flamboyant. They'd have doubles here for everybody. I'm sort of renegade as far as that goes. I like to use actors, because I think the audience wants to see the actor. They're not paying to see the stunt guys. They're paying to see the actors."

The brothers embrace.

>   WYATT
>   (laughing)
> That's right. Morgan, meet Marshal
> Meagher.

>   MORGAN
> Nice to meet ya.

>   MEAGHER
> You too. Now take off those guns.

>   MORGAN
> Do what?

Morgan checks with Wyatt to see if Meagher's
kidding.

>   WYATT
> Take off the guns.

Morgan unbuckles.

>   WYATT
> When'd you get to town?

>   MORGAN
> About an hour ago.

>   WYATT
>   (to Meagher)
> This boy would make a hell of a deputy.

>   MEAGHER
> Might have an opening sometime. If we
> do, he can put 'em back on.

>   WYATT
> It's really good to see you, Morg.

>   MORGAN
> I got something to show you.

INT. STAIRWELL/SECOND FLOOR, WICHITA HOTEL—NIGHT
Morgan excitedly leads Wyatt up the steps. They
approach a doorway near the top of the stairs.

>   MORGAN
> You're not gonna believe this, Wyatt.
> Hold on to your hat…or maybe just take
> it off.

Morgan raps on the door, then immediately
sticks his head in.

*Linden Ashby as Morgan Earp and
Alison Elliott as Lou.*

>   MORGAN
> You decent, hon? Here he is…

Morgan throws open the door and motions
Wyatt inside.

INT. HOTEL ROOM—NIGHT
Standing at an open suitcase on the bed is a
beautiful, innocent young woman in her early
twenties, LOU (LOUISA HOUSTON). She
smiles shyly at Wyatt.

>   MORGAN
> Lou, this is him…this is my big brother.

Morgan watches Wyatt's face to gauge his appre-
ciation of this pretty young prize. He's not dis-
appointed. Wyatt gives Morgan an approving
glance as he steps forward to offer his hand.

>   WYATT
> How do you do, ma'am.

>   LOU
> It's a pleasure to meet you, James.

>   MORGAN
> This is Wyatt, not James. We'll find
> James later.

Morgan puts a proud arm around Lou.

MORGAN
Lou and I met out in California when I went to see the folks. Isn't she the sweetest thing you ever seen?

Lou blushes and elbows Morgan. Wyatt laughs softly, but there is melancholy in his eyes; her freshness reminds him of Urilla.

WYATT
I believe she is.
(a thought occurs)
Say, are you two…?

MORGAN
As good as, I guess. I'd fight any man that said different. But you didn't miss any wedding, if that's what you're worried about.

Lou picks up some clothes and turns away, embarrassed.

MORGAN
I can't wait to show her off to James. Can you take us to him?

WYATT
So you haven't met Bessie yet?

MORGAN
(first he's heard the name)
Bessie? Has James got himself a sweet little bride, too?

WYATT
(thinks about it a moment)
As good as, I guess…

EXT. MAIN STREET, WICHITA—DAY
Wyatt rides into town after a long trip. On horses behind him, two handcuffed Fugitives.

From the sidewalk, a Huge Man, 300 pounds of him, watches with interest and wipes his sweaty brow.

CHERYL CARASIK, SET DECORATOR

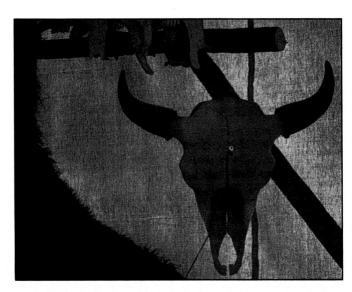

CARASIK ON THE PROCESS OF THE SET DECORATOR

The production designer and the set decorator talk a lot, and then we break down the script. I read it as a decorator and also as a part of the art department, just reading for the whole feeling, the color palette and what the general flavor is going to be. And then my process usually begins with talking to the designer, in this case talking to Ida and talking to Larry. We formulate a vision. Then we do our own research. I research my own interior decorating, and Ida does more general research. And through the script and direction from Larry, we come up with these ideas.

"The designer and the decorator, if they're going to have a good-looking set, they're going to have a lot of communication between them. [The designer decides on] the walls, the paint, the floors, the wallpapers, the construction, etc. Then I proceed with my detailing with fabrics, pictures, fixtures, furniture—the styling of the room. I say, this chair would look really great here or this fabric is going to contrast so much with the wallpaper, and it's going to look great. We have to think about lighting. I decorate anamorphically. How am I going to compose this wall, so I get what I want out of it and what Larry needs?

"When I first met Ida, I told her that I really wanted to take this movie to another level. I wanted to really push the envelope. I wanted to be completely correct in the period, but I also wanted to push the look, in my fabrics, in my colors, in my silhouettes or certain pieces of furniture. A chair against the wall and a picture above it can be a piece of art to me all by itself. The simplicity of that is beautiful, and Larry gets it. He understands that, which is so beautiful. And Ida knows that. The simplicity of a room is just as beautiful as a cluttered room. There's beauty in both."

THE MANY SALOONS OF WYATT EARP

We have 11 or 12 saloons in this movie. Each one has a theme and they all look different. That's a real anchor for me, to be able to kick off of that theme. For instance, Lucky's was our first saloon. We had the boxing theme in Lucky's

Saloon because we had the boxing out in front. In the Campbell Hatch, I had the fan motif. The Pryor's Saloon has the steer horn theme, which is something that we actually took from the research. The Fort Griffin tent-saloon has a lot of flags in it, period flags for Texas. The Oriental was the beauty set. The Comique will be a theatrical theme because there is a stage in there."

THE IMPORTANCE OF DETAIL

I like to be able to put buttons in a sewing box if it's on a table, because that's what it is. It's a sewing box and it would have buttons and threads and needles in it, even though no one's ever going to open it. It's no longer a set to me. It becomes a living space. In Urilla's house, for instance, there were flowers and there was food on the table. There were fresh pies and fresh bread sitting on the table in the background because that's what they had. A lot of people say to me, 'Why are you bothering with detail on this so much? You're never going to see that.' That isn't the issue. If we see it, that's icing on the cake for me."

THE SCOPE OF WYATT EARP

When Ida asked me to do the movie, I accepted it with open arms, but I was petrified by the immensity of the sets. There are over ninety sets in the breakdown, which is very hard on the set-decorating crew because you're coming and going so fast. We have distances to travel and we have to dress and we have to strike and we have to be ahead of [the shooting crew]. One set after another keeps coming. I mean, there is no down time for us. Right now the company's here, but I'm already working on [the Dodge City set]. [The Wichita set] is dressed. That's where the company is shooting next. It's finished. You could go see it tomorrow if you wanted to. But I can't think about that. That's done. That's history. Even though it hasn't been shot yet, I have to go to Dodge and get Dodge ready because that's where they're shooting next week. In the meantime, I have to come back and open Larry in every set, to make sure everything's okay. So I've made three trips to Dodge today, back and forth. That is the pace of the movie. There are always five big things going on.

"I think that on this movie, I've been

the most challenged in my career. This is the most incredible film I've ever worked on, with the best crew. I'm so proud to be a part of it. I think it's going to go down in history as a great piece of filmmaking. I really believe that."

KASDAN ON CARASIK

Cheryl's the best set decorator I've had the good fortune to work with. She has incredible interest in the details which make great set decoration. You can't walk onto a set that she's decorated without seeing a million little details that the camera will never see, but which are immensely helpful to the actors and to me, to just immerse everybody working there in a sense of veracity. She's a workaholic in terms of getting the right detail, the right piece of furniture, the right fabric. She brings to it, like Ida, impeccable taste. And on top of that she's incredibly

practical. She's never late. She's never unprepared. She's always ahead of us, in the best way, the way they're supposed to be but sometimes aren't. Cheryl is the best combination I've had of talent, taste, and pragmatic efficiency."

EXT. CITY JAIL—DAY
Wyatt comes out and starts down the sidewalk.
Several Citizens greet him as he goes, but he's
too tired to give much of a response. He turns
down an alley rubbing at the back of his sore
neck.

> VOICE (OS)
> (huge and gruff)
> Wyatt Earp!

Wyatt does not hesitate. He spins and draws.
It's the first time we've seen him do this and it's
too fast to see it even now. His Colt is simply in
his hand, up and cocked.

The Huge Man we saw before is standing at the
end of the alley, practically filling it with his immense bulk. He smiles at what he's just seen as
he raises both his hands in innocence. His name
is LARRY DEGER.

> DEGER
> (laughing)
> Don't shoot. If you missed me it'd destroy
> your reputation.

> WYATT
> (unamused, lowers his gun)
> Mister, I ain't in the mood…

Deger slowly lowers his left hand to his coat
and pulls it back to reveal a badge.

> DEGER
> Larry Deger, from Dodge City. People tell
> me you're the man I'm lookin' for.

EXT. BIG TREE CORRAL, EDGE OF
WICHITA—DAY
The oldest, biggest tree in Wichita creates cool
shade next to a large corral milling with horses.
Out beyond the corral are the open grasslands
of Kansas. It's a pretty spot. Wyatt and Deger
lean against the fence in the shade, Wyatt looking off toward the open spaces.

> DEGER
> …the Chisholm Trail is dying. They
> won't be bringing the big herds to
> Wichita anymore. Now that there's a
> railhead in Dodge City, the Texans are
> running their beeves up across the
> Nations to the Cimarron.

> WYATT
> Folks in Dodge must be mighty pleased.

> DEGER
> Most of 'em. Not me. We used to see
> thirty thousand head of cattle come
> through in a season. This year looks
> closer to three hundred thousand.
> (Wyatt reacts)
> Think about it…

> WYATT
> That's a lot of drunk cowboys.

DEGER
Oh, that's just the start of it. With all that money floatin' in, you can guess the crowd that followed.

WYATT
How much?

DEGER
Seventy-five a month...

WYATT
I'm making more than that here.

DEGER
...plus two dollars and fifty cents for every arrest.

Wyatt reacts big to that; his eyes light up.

DEGER
I need help and lots of it. Things are already out of hand. The Mayor and the City Council have authorized me to get it.

WYATT
So you're looking for more than one?

DEGER
Hell, yes! You know anyone you can trust?

Wyatt looks out at the western horizon, in the direction of Dodge City. A smile comes slowly to his face.

WYATT
I might know a few.

EXT. PLAINS OUTSIDE OF DODGE CITY—MAGIC HOUR
Cattle. Thousands of head. Far as the eye can see. Scattered Cowboys on horseback ride night duty, keeping them together.

EXT. STOCKYARDS, DODGE CITY—NIGHT
More cattle. Thousands more. Every pen is full to bursting. The railroad track with its idle trains runs along one side. We begin to HEAR

distant GUNSHOTS and WHOOPS and other ASSORTED HUBBUB.

EXT. FRONT STREET, DODGE CITY—
NIGHT
CLOSE ON a sign—"Welcome to DODGE CITY, KANSAS. No carrying of firearms within the City Limits." The sign is being hammered into the ground with the butt of a shotgun.

Front Street is the busiest street in the busiest cowtown in America. There are a dozen saloons and two dozen brothels to serve the Cowboys, Freighters, Hunters, Scouts, Gamblers, Confidence Men, Prostitutes, Railroaders and Troublemakers who jam the area.

What once seemed just raucous has now crossed the line into chaos and anarchy. Right now the Trail Crew of the Clements Brothers' cattle drive is moving down Front Street. They've just arrived in town and they're giving it a huge,

ear-shattering "Hurrah." They're WHOOP-ING like banshees. Six-guns and Winchesters are BLASTING—mostly skyward, but a fair percentage hitting buildings, sidewalks and windows. Only luck that no one is dead just yet.

MANNEN CLEMENTS himself, a big, bearded Texan, is near the front of the 50-man parade of tumult. At his side, his brother and foreman, GYP CLEMENTS. They're smiling hugely at the shenanigans of their wild boys. Suddenly, just in front of Clements, a SHOTGUN BLASTS toward the heavens. It is so loud and so close that, even in this cacophony, it commands attention.

Standing alone, in the middle of the street, shotgun raised, is Wyatt. He wears a longish black coat, white shirt and black string tie. And, of course, a badge. Relative QUIET has descended on the immediate area.

WYATT

I'm Wyatt Earp.

There is a long moment of quiet. It spreads rapidly back through the Trail Crew; some move their horses up for a closer look, some dismount and lead their horses up onto the sidewalks to get a clearer view of the action.

MANNEN

Who?

WYATT

Wyatt Earp.

Mannen and Gyp exchange surprised looks, then peer more closely at the figure down in front of them. Finally, Gyp speaks loudly to Mannen—

GYP

Who the fuck is Wyatt Earp?

COWBOY ON FOOT

Looks to me like just some asshole.

Morgan steps from the shadows behind this unlucky fellow and clubs him over the head with one of the two Colts in his hands. There is a stir among the Trail Crew, but now they're unsure where the opposition might come from.

MORGAN

He's the asshole who enforces the law.

GYP

There ain't no law in Dodge City…not for the Clements crew.

WYATT

We've got some new laws since you boys were here. Tell 'em, Morgan.

MORGAN

All visitors must check their guns immediately upon arrival.

GYP

That'll be the day!

Virgil steps to the rail of a second-floor porch. He's wearing a badge and cradling a scatter gun.

VIRGIL

No discharge of firearms within the city limits…'cept on the Fourth of July and Christmas Day.

A Cowboy sits on his horse on the wooden sidewalk. Huge Larry Deger appears and pokes the horse roughly in its flank with his rifle. The horse springs off the sidewalk in a panic, throwing the Cowboy.

"I'M WYATT EARP." "WHO?" "WYATT EARP."

By Dodge City, Wyatt has become the man he's going to be, but without the reputation. It's the man without a mustache. He's not famous enough yet for one of the Clements crew to say to the boss, 'Quiet, stupid. That's Wyatt Earp.'

"Wyatt found a way to get his point across. He didn't do it by reputation. He did it with a really calculating chess move—by saying, 'Do you yield?' It was like something that would happen 200 years ago, with a sword. 'Do you yield? If you don't yield, I'm going to run you through. And if you do yield, then we'll just call it a day. We'll call it even. And you'll understand from now on who I am, and I'll understand who you are. And if we're not friends, then let's be clear about who I am and who you are, and the next time we meet, there won't be any talking.'"
—KEVIN COSTNER

Wyatt's story is one of a good prospect for becoming a certain kind of man, who then does all the things to become that kind of man. And all those things have to do with courage and calm in the face of danger and deliberateness about his actions. [These were the issues] in the buffalo hunting and in law enforcement as well.

"I think that what happens in Dodge is that he becomes the man that eventually goes to Tombstone. Up to that point he's evolving as a lawman, and his ideas about how to do the job are evolving. What happens with the Clements crew is a pivotal incident for him in terms of testing his methods against the world and against the real danger. And he succeeds. I think it seals for him the idea that if you do the job a certain way, you can be effective. But it requires enormous courage to do it. And confidence. And that's what develops in Dodge City."
—LAWRENCE KASDAN

DEGER

No animals on the sidewalks…no riding *into* stores, saloons, dancehalls or gamblin' houses. No public intoxication.

After a moment, this causes a wave of amusement among the Clements crew.

GYP

Mannen, what's that supposed to mean…public intoxication?

MANNEN

Maybe it means we done enough talkin'.

WYATT

Nope…that means if you do anything we don't much approve of, we got a legal right to shoot you down.

MANNEN

Are you the one that's gonna try?

Wyatt, casually cradling the shotgun, looks at him a moment, then walks the ten feet to Mannen's horse, so he's right below the cattleman. He speaks very softly.

I always disliked beating up the general run of cowboys, and I could handle many of them without employing extreme measures. But at this particular time their long period of license had made the whole crowd so unruly that the only way to get the situation in hand was to knock over every man who looked twice at me."
—WYATT EARP

Take it from me, no one has ever humiliated this man Earp, nor made him show the white feather under any circumstances whatever. While he is now a man past sixty, there are still a great many so-called bad men in this country who would be found, if put to the test, to be much easier game to tackle than this same lean and lanky Earp…" —BAT MASTERSON

WYATT

Mr. Clements, your men respect you, and I don't want to do anything to take away from that. I'm sure you've earned it. So you and your boys are welcome in Dodge City as long as you obey the law.
(looks around a moment)
But if you don't want to cooperate, I'm gonna let you have it with this shotgun right now…and it'll open you up so wide, your whole crew is gonna see what you had for breakfast.
(he glances over at Gyp)
After that, it won't matter much what happens next, will it?

Mannen reacts, but he keeps it to himself. He looks down at Wyatt a long time, making the decision of a lifetime. Finally, he lets out a great roar of a laugh; to anyone out of earshot, he seems master of the situation. He turns his horse to speak to his men, as he unbuckles his holster.

MANNEN

Give up your guns, boys. The only ones you'll need tonight are sittin' right between your legs!

There's some laughter, some surprise, and a lot of curiosity among the Trail Crew, but they do as they're told. Wyatt exchanges a look with his brothers as the lawmen begin to collect weapons.

INT. RESTAURANT (SIX MONTHS LATER)—DAY
EXTREME CLOSEUP on a dish, the remains of a breakfast. Hands put down knife and fork, and lift a white napkin. We TILT UP to a CLOSE SHOT of Wyatt, wiping his mouth. When he takes the napkin away, we see for the first time the full mustache curving down around his mouth.

Morgan, Virgil, and Bat and Ed Masterson are at the table with Wyatt. The Mastersons have seasoned quite a bit since we last saw them. Bat, in particular, has the air of a formidable man.

WYATT

The job don't pay a salary to start.

BAT
No salary?

WYATT
Pays two dollars and fifty cents for every arrest.

MORGAN
Wyatt cleared, what, a thousand dollars last month.

ED
Hell, how many is that?

VIRGIL
A lot.

BAT
You got yourself a bit of a reputation, Wyatt.

WYATT
Tricky thing, the reputation business, Bat.

ED
I got to tell you, Wyatt, not all a man hears is good. We heard about you all the way over in Abilene.

MORGAN
(pleased)
What are they sayin'?

ED
They say people in Dodge are complainin' you're too quick to bash a man just 'cause you don't like the way he looks.

MORGAN
(mock angry)
Tell me what sonuvabitch is complainin'…I'll go bash 'em.

Ed throws him an impatient look.

MORGAN
I know plenty of people that like Wyatt around here. Let's see…there's me, there's Virgil…
(thinking hard)
…there's me…

Wyatt and Morgan both laugh.

EXT. FRONT STREET—NIGHT
Morgan makes his way down the busy sidewalk. He has his usual restless energy and easy smile, but his eyes miss nothing as he makes his rounds.

From left, Morgan, Wyatt, Ed and Bat Masterson, and Michael Madsen as Virgil Earp

Now he nods at someone out in the street and we leave him and pick up—

Wyatt, Ed Masterson and Bat Masterson walking in the other direction down the street. All three men wear badges and are armed. Coming down the street toward them are two Drunken Cowboys, who have just left a saloon. Both men are armed. Wyatt looks over at the Mastersons.

> WYATT
> Well, you might as well get broke in sometime. Why don't you boys handle this one.

Wyatt steps off into the shadows. Ed and Bat exchange a look as the two drunks approach. Ed smiles at the men and tips his derby.

> ED
> Evenin'.

They ignore him and keep walking.

> ED
> Looks like you boys been doin' some drinkin'.

> COWBOY #1
> (turns and belches at Ed)
> What makes you say that?

"I'M ED MASTERSON. THIS IS MY BROTHER." "...BAT."

I read a book called *Bat Masterson*. I got real curious about him because he was an interesting historic figure and I was playing him. He was quite a dandy. Initially he was a young kid who wanted to do his thing in the West. Then he became a lawman with Wyatt. He was quite a storyteller. There are lots of legends about him. They say that he killed 26 people. I told Larry that and he said, 'He probably never killed anybody.' Which could be true; there were a lot of tall tales. He definitely killed one guy, though. They were in love with the same woman in Texas, Molly Brennan, and there was a a shoot-out over her. Bat killed the man, but he got shot in the left leg. He walked with a limp for the rest of his life and used a cane. That's why in the famous pictures of Bat with his hat and his mustache he has a cane.

"After Wyatt left for Tombstone, Bat stayed in Dodge City for a while before moving to New York City. He was quite a guy. He wasn't educated initially, but he was self-taught. He became a sports writer and lived a long time.

"Bat wrote the first account of Wyatt. He was really taken with Wyatt because he felt Wyatt was the best man he had ever met. He said things like that. 'He was a man of steel, a man of resolve.' Bat always admired Wyatt and he helped begin the legend through the essays he wrote for the newspaper."

—TOM SIZEMORE (BAT MASTERSON)

I think that maybe Ed was ahead of his time. When I really had my feathers up, I announced, 'Ed is the new West!' But in milder moments, I would say, he was ahead of his time. He had a sense that money could be made with land, and that the inevitable development of the West required a whole lot of people to come out, common people, the big bulk of people who like not to be threatened and who like to have secu-

rity and who don't like to be tested every day for their masculinity, or whatever. Those kinds of people needed a sense of law and order that was more in keeping with what their morality was, and in that way Ed had a personality and a sense of justice that suited them. It's true that when Ed was shot, they turned out in that town unlike they ever had before. For two days they were in

mourning, and they had black bunting on everything. They grieved for him. He was a leader and he was well liked.

"Wyatt is representative of a very tough order in the West that was required when the frontier was trying to turn itself from being a lawless, chaotic place into a place where you could actually get farmers to stay and get them to build churches and develop roots, which businessmen needed in order to sell their wares. The community needed more and more gentle people to come and not be intimidated by the endless flow of cow herds and the cowboys that came through driving them. Wyatt was crucial to turning that around in the West, but the future of the West lay in gentler lawkeeping practices. And I think Ed was ahead of his time."

—BILL PULLMAN (ED MASTERSON)

In addition to being important friends to Wyatt during that period of his life, the Mastersons represent the two poles in him. Ed is kind of innocent and Bat is much more like the finished Wyatt, sort of pragmatic and tougher. Ed represents a kind of naivete which is deadly and which Wyatt has come out of. You could say that Ed is a kind of liberal lawman and Wyatt is much more conservative, a hard-liner. And given the circumstances, it seems the more appropriate approach." —LAWRENCE KASDAN

ED
Just intuition I guess. Anyways, I'm glad you're havin' a good time, but you know there's a city ordinance against wearing firearms in town.

Both Cowboys have now stopped and turned to face the Mastersons. Their look is ugly.

COWBOY #2
Says who?

BAT
(steely)
Says the law, that's who.

The two Cowboys tense in a drunken preparation for a fight. Ed, wanting to calm things, turns to Bat.

ED
Now, Bat, you're bein' about as sociable as an ulcerated molar. These boys don't want—

Wyatt appears from the shadows and whacks first one, then the other Drunken Cowboy over the head with his gun barrel. Bat immediately

draws his gun to cover Wyatt. Ed is shocked. Movement on the street slows to take in the action. Several Cowboys and Townspeople are clearly disapproving of Wyatt's methods.

ED
Holy shit, Wyatt!

Wyatt is bending to relieve the first Cowboy of his gun. He looks up at Ed, angry.

WYATT
You talk too much, Ed.

ED
You didn't have to do that, Wyatt.

Wyatt has moved to the second Cowboy. He pries open his hand; there is a small-caliber pistol in it. Even Wyatt is surprised.

ED
I'll be a son of a…

BAT
(looks at Wyatt)
I was standing right here. I didn't see it either.

INT. DODGE CITY JAIL—NIGHT
Wyatt, Ed and Bat come out of the cellblock,
where they've deposited the Drunken Cowboys.

ED
You know that fella coulda gone for his
gun after he saw you buffalo his friend.

WYATT
Maybe.

ED
He was so drunk he couldn't have hit the
ground with his hat in three tries.
        (Wyatt and Bat don't respond)
I'm just sayin', I believe I coulda talked
those guns off'em.

WYATT
Ed, if I were you, I'd look for another line
of work. Politics maybe.

BAT
Ed's got a different style is all, Wyatt.
People like it.

WYATT
You could get killed in this line of work,
Ed. You could get people around you
killed.

BAT
Wyatt, we're just getting started.

WYATT
I know. And when I hit that fella, Bat,
your first instinct was to pull your
weapon and cover me. Ed, this is a harsh
land. It doesn't suffer fools.

Wyatt doesn't suffer fools gladly. With Ed Masterson, it no longer matters what their history was. Their friendship falls into
the background. Wyatt lays it out for him. He says, 'You talk too
much.' I think it's a very important scene, because the relationship
doesn't matter anymore. Suddenly Ed is seeing a different human
being. And when Ed thinks he can change Wyatt's mind in the next
scene, Wyatt says, 'You're not a deliberate man, Ed.' This was confusing for Bat. I don't believe Bat would let Wyatt hit his brother but,
on the other hand, he valued what Wyatt said. He understood it. I
think that's always the appeal of somebody who's very direct. They
can be very difficult to deal with and you may wish that they had a
subtlety about them, but if you can eventually get past their gruffness,
you find that directness very refreshing."
                                                    —KEVIN COSTNER

ED
I'm not a fool, Wyatt.

WYATT
No, you're not. But you're not a deliberate man, Ed. I don't sense that about
you. You're too…affable.

INT. MATTIE'S ROOM—DAY
Midday. The cramped room of a prostitute
named MATTIE. She lies in bed, watching
Wyatt get dressed. She's crazy in love with him.
He takes some money from his pants and dis-
creetly lays it on the dresser.

MATTIE
Don't do that, Wyatt. Please. You know
how I feel.

WYATT
I want to, Mattie.

MATTIE
I could make you happy, Wyatt, if you'd
give me the chance. I know I could.

Wyatt turns to look at her.

WYATT
I care for you, Mattie. But I'm not going
to tell you things that aren't so.
        (she winces)
I don't want to cause you pain, Mattie. If
seeing me causes you pain…

MATTIE
        (alarmed)
No, Wyatt… we have time. I have to
give you time…you'll see. I can be anything you want me to be.

Wyatt accepts that gently, not giving much.

MATTIE
…Only, don't leave money on my dresser,
please…unless…unless it's cause you
want to take care of me. Is that how you
mean it, Wyatt?

Wyatt looks at her a long time before nodding
slightly, a little sadly.

EXT. STREET OUTSIDE BOARDING
HOUSE—DAY
Wyatt comes out of Mattie's place, a distracted
look on his face. Ed and Bat wait uncomfortably
on the sidewalk for him.

WYATT

Hi, guys.

BAT

Wyatt...the Mayor's asked us to come get you.

WYATT

The Mayor? Something goin' on?

Bat seems uneasy; he shuffles and stares at the ground.

ED

There's been some kind of meeting with Mayor Kelly.

WYATT

About what?

BAT

We weren't there, Wyatt.

ED

Some people are concerned with the way you've been runnin' things, Wyatt.

Ed glances at Bat, who wants no part of this.

WYATT

What do you think, Ed?

ED

(pained by this)
There's been some complaints.

WYATT

From some in jail, maybe. Not from citizens.

ED

Some of them, too...I'm just sayin' this out of friendship, Wyatt. So you know. I talk to a lot of people.

Wyatt stares at Bat.

BAT

All I know is the Mayor wants to see you. He asked us to find you. That's what we did.

EXT. FLATLANDS, NORTHERN TEXAS—DAY

Wyatt rides alone across the dry, hard Texas landscape.

Mare Winningham as Mattie

EXT. MAIN DRAG, FORT GRIFFIN, TEXAS—DAY

There's a large cavalry post here, and an obvious presence of uniformed Soldiers, around which has sprung up a dusty little town to meet their needs. Wyatt rides into town, covered with the grime of his journey. One of the wooden structures displays a sign: SHANSSEY'S SALOON. Wyatt dismounts in front and goes inside.

INT. SHANSSEY'S SALOON—DAY

The proprietor of this place is the same John Shanssey whom Wyatt saved from permanent damage back in the prize fight in the Railway Camp many years before. He and Wyatt are sharing a laugh over the bar in the nearly deserted saloon.

SHANSSEY

...You know Donovan went all the way to a title shot after that bout. I don't know what shape I'd be in today if you hadn't stopped that fight...
    (Wyatt shrugs)
...probably be running a crappy saloon in some feedbag town...

Shanssey laughs loudest at his own joke, but Wyatt joins him. Shanssey offers again to pour some whiskey for Wyatt, but Wyatt raises a hand to demur.

SHANSSEY
(frowns, pours himself one)
What are you doin' in these parts? I thought you was Deputy Marshal in Dodge.

WYATT
I was till the city fathers forgot to renew my contract. Too much of a hard ass, I guess.

SHANSSEY
Well, you are, Wyatt. Everybody knows that. Who's replaced you?

WYATT
A fella named Masterson.

SHANSSEY
Bat Masterson?

WYATT
No, his brother Ed.

SHANSSEY
What's he like?

WYATT
Affable. Very affable.

SHANSSEY
What're you up to?

WYATT
Doing a job for the railroad. Looking for a fellow name of Dave Rudabaugh. I heard he might be headed this way.

SHANSSEY
He come through here all right, but where he went I couldn't tell ya. What'd he do?

WYATT
Robbed the Sante Fe train…three times, it looks like.

SHANSSEY
(ponders that, gets a thought)
There's somebody who might know something. If he does, he'll probably tell ya. He hates Rudabaugh. Name's Doc Holliday.

WYATT
(reacts)
He's a killer, isn't he?

SHANSSEY

He's killed some. He owes me a couple favors and he's good as his word. Travels with a whore name of Big Nose Kate, but he's not her pimp.

INT. TENT SALOON—DAY

There's light coming through the fabric of the large tent, giving the whole place a slightly unearthly quality. It's very quiet in here at midday. Shanssey and Wyatt come in. Shanssey looks, then leads Wyatt across the tent.

Sitting alone at a table in the corner, playing solitaire, is DOC HOLLIDAY. He's a couple years younger than Wyatt, but you wouldn't know it to look at him. He's wasting away with tuberculosis. On the table is a bottle of whiskey and a glass.

SHANSSEY

Doc.

DOC

(doesn't look up)

John.

SHANSSEY

I'd like you to meet a friend of mine… Wyatt Earp.

DOC

(still looking at his cards)

…Wyatt Earp…I've heard that name somewhere…don't know where, but it wasn't good.

SHANSSEY

Mind if we sit down?

Doc finally looks up from his cards. He looks straight into Wyatt's eyes. For a long time. Saying nothing. Finally he nods. The two men sit. Doc goes back to his game.

WYATT

I'm looking for Dave Rudabaugh. There's a reward for information about him if it leads to his arrest.

DOC

You a lawman, Wyatt Earp?

(Wyatt nods)

You're not wearing a badge. Are you ashamed of your profession? I myself was a dentist. And I was proud to be a dentist.

DOC (cont'd)

I did not hide the fact that I was a dentist. How are your teeth, Wyatt Earp?

WYATT

They're working all right, I guess.

DOC

Take good care of them. They can't be replaced. I am no longer a dentist. I am a sporting man. That is my work now. In Georgia we were taught a man should take pride in his work. Ever been to Georgia, Wyatt Earp?

(Wyatt shakes his head)

Beautiful state, Georgia. Very green. I was forced to leave Georgia. And I fear I'll never see it again.

WYATT

I'm sorry.

Wyatt says this with real sincerity, and that seems to stop Doc. He puts his cards down and looks at Wyatt. Without taking his eyes off Wyatt, he reaches for the whiskey bottle and knocks it over. Wyatt's hand flashes out and catches the bottle before a drop is spilled. He sets is gently upright in front of Doc, who looks from the bottle to Wyatt. After several beats—

DOC

Do you believe in friendship, Wyatt Earp?

Wyatt looks at him a long moment, then nods.

DOC

So do I. Do you have many friends?

Wyatt shakes his head "no." Doc indicates Shanssey.

DOC

John has been a friend to me when most men would not. Dave Rudabaugh is an ignorant scoundrel. I disapprove of his very existence. I considered ending it on several occasions, but self-control got the better of me. Besides, I am a sporting man, not a killer.

With that, he begins to cough. It grows. First he uses his right hand to cover his mouth, then pulls a handkerchief from his pocket. He pours himself some whiskey and gulps it down. The cough subsides raggedly. When he has caught his breath, he acts as though the episode never happened.

DOC

Tell me about the reward, Wyatt Earp.

WYATT

You'd be doing me a favor if you would call me either Wyatt or Earp, not both.

Doc looks at him a moment and smiles; he's been waiting for this.

DOC

All right…Wyatt. Call me Doc.

He offers Wyatt his right hand, to shake. Without hesitation, Wyatt takes it.

INT. COMIQUE THEATRE AND SALOON
—NIGHT
Five Cowboys are having a drunken good time at the bar. One of them, WAGNER, is wearing a gun.

Ed Masterson comes in the front door. He exchanges a meaningful look with the Bartender and walks up behind Wagner. After a moment, the drunken Cowboy reads his friends' expression and turns to look at Ed.

ED

Howdy, friend.

"While he never did anything to entitle him to a statue in the Hall of Fame, Doc Holliday was nevertheless a most picturesque character on the western border in those days when the pistol instead of law courts determined issues. Holliday was a product of the state of Georgia, and a scion of a most respectable and prominent family. He graduated as a dentist from one of the medical colleges of his native state before he left it, but did not follow his profession very long after receiving his diploma. It was perhaps too respectable a calling for him…

"Holliday seemed to be absolutely unable to keep out of trouble for any great length of time. He would no sooner be out of one scrape before he was in another, and the strange part of it is he was more often in the right than in the wrong, which has rarely ever been the case with a man who is continually getting himself into trouble."
—BAT MASTERSON

"CALL ME DOC."

QUAID ON DOC

In legend anyway, Doc Holliday was bigger than life. [The real John Holliday] was a dentist, but he stopped practicing dentistry because of his tuberculosis. He was well-educated. He understood Latin, the sciences, literature. He was a southerner and although there were a lot of southerners out west, I think being from the south gave him a certain flair, a certain romanticism.

"He was told when he contracted tuberculosis that he had two years to live, and that if he wanted to make it those two years he should move to the high plateaus of the West, because the air was better for his condition. So he moved out west and surprised himself by living another fourteen years. He drank about two quarts of whiskey a day, about a pint of whiskey just to get up in the morning, because it was such a struggle for him to breathe. He couldn't practice dentistry, because he'd cough all

ON TRANSFORMING INTO DOC

I'm the kind of actor where, when I get a part, especially a historical part, I feel as if I owe it to that person to try to be as close to them as I can within the context of the story. That's why I lost all this weight. I started at 182. I'm down to 139. That's just the way I do it.

"The way I look at it, I can't go back and reshoot it. And it's not like I can't eat for the rest of my life. It's just a few months. Larry's been sweating over this thing for a year. Kevin's had this project for a long time. This is my work. Twenty years from now, I'm the one who's going to have to live with my work."

KASDAN ON CASTING QUAID

I've admired Dennis's work for a long time. I thought he was spectacular in *The Right Stuff* and really moving in *Everybody's All American*. I think he's just a terrific actor with a lot of charisma on the screen. That's a big combination, really skilled actor and very charismatic. That's what I needed for Doc. And I went to see large sections of *Flesh and Bone*, which Steve Kloves was editing, and he was terrific in it, really austere and economical. He achieved his effects in a very simple way. He trusted himself to be that person without very much showy stuff. Even though Doc is a very showy part, the quality that I'm attracted to in actors is always simplicity. I knew that he could be flashy. That's what the part in *The Right Stuff* is about, but to see that he could be simple and strong, that was very encouraging.

"When he first came in to see me, he was thirty-five pounds heavier. He said, 'Do you want me to lose weight?' And I said, 'That would be great.' But I wasn't talking about what he eventually did, and what he did has been extraordinary. It tells you a lot about his approach to the role. Not only does he look exactly like the real John Holliday, but he's obviously totally committed to the part. He's worked hard on his accent and he's obviously sacrificed a lot for his body. That kind of commitment [to the movie] is an inspiration to everybody."

over his patients, so he became a gambler, basically to earn his keep, to make a living. As a gambler he got into altercations so he learned how to use a firearm, he carried a knife

"I think that what he hated most in the world was ignorance, and there was a lot of that out west. He longed for the softer things in life, and there were not many people around to really talk about the softer things, the greater things. I think that's one of the reasons he and Wyatt were friends—Doc loved the conversation.

"I think Doc lived by his reputation more than by his skills. His reputation

protected him because if you have a tough reputation, you don't have to get in too many fights. A fourteen-year-old boy could beat this guy up. People say he was a great gunfighter, and he probably was. What made him a great gunfighter, I think, was the fact that in a gunfight—think about it, put yourself in that situation—you're going to draw and shoot off as many as you can. The one who's not going to miss is the guy who takes deliberate aim and stands there. The guy who has nothing to lose has the best chance to live. Doc had nothing to lose. He had given up on life."

WAGNER
You ain't my friend.

ED
True enough. But I am the law here, and
the law says you can't wear your gun in
town. Hand it over.

WAGNER
What if I don't?

Ed frowns. He eyes Wagner's friends, who, like
everyone else in the saloon, are now watching
the confrontation.

ED
I'll take it away from you. You'll go to jail
and miss the party. You don't want that
now, do you?

WAGNER
What's your name?

ED
Masterson.

Wagner reacts to the name, as do his friends.
Suddenly, Ed shouts at him, causing Wagner to
jump—

ED
Give it to me!

Wagner hands over the gun. Ed gives it to the
Bartender, who stows it away under the bar.

ED
(to Bartender)
Don't give it back till they're leavin'
town.
(smiles at Wagner)
Thank you.

Ed goes to the door and out, but never lets the
Cowboys out of his view. One of Wagner's
friends, Walker, looks at him and laughs. Wagner scowls.

EXT. COMIQUE THEATRE AND SALOON
—NIGHT
Ed is on the sidewalk just outside the swinging
doors. He's been speaking to a Citizen, who
now moves off. Ed catches something out of the
corner of his eye a second before Wagner bursts
out of the doors, pulling a pistol from inside his
coat. Ed is able to grab Wagner just as he brings
up the gun and together they slam back against
the front wall of the saloon, grappling. A mass
of humanity begins to flow through the saloon
doors and out onto the street. But suddenly—

Wagner strains and gets some air between himself and Ed. He gets the pistol up into Ed's side

and FIRES. The crowd scatters. Ed is blown across the sidewalk, his coat erupting in flame. By the time he hits the ground, his Colt is out and BLASTING. Wagner is hit in the chest and thrown against the wall; his gun CLATTERS to the sidewalk. It all happens very fast.

Ed, grimacing, is swatting at the flames on his coat when he sees Walker pick up his friend's fallen gun and lift the barrel toward him. Ed FIRES twice more, hitting Walker both times. Walker goes down.

Now it's quiet. The surrounding crowd seems not to know what to do. Ed struggles to his feet, his coat now smoldering. Holding his side, he stumbles out into the street and WE STAY WITH HIM. He staggers down the street, looking as if he might go down at any moment. But he doesn't; he just keeps on going. It's interminable—agonizing to watch.

Bat comes around the corner on the run. He sees his brother and hurries to him. Ed stumbles into his arms.

> ED
> Bat, I'm shot.

Ed dies in his brother's embrace.

> BAT
> Ed...oh god.

EXT. MAIN DRAG, FORT GRIFFIN—DAY
Wyatt rides into town. On a horse behind him, a handcuffed Dave Rudabaugh.

INT. WESTERN UNION OFFICE, FORT GRIFFIN—DAY
Wyatt stands reading a telegram. We see the words in EXTREME CLOSEUP. The telegram is addressed to Wyatt care of the Sante Fe Railroad head office, but the words that matter are these—

"Marshal Ed Masterson murdered by cowboys. Lawlessness near riot proportions. Request you return immediately to Dodge City. Will renew contract as Assistant City Marshal at double salary. Signed, James Kelly, Mayor."

"The death of Ed Masterson reinforces Wyatt's idea that there aren't a lot of ways to do the job, that it can't be done in half measures. It's all or nothing, like his father said, swing to hit, hit to kill. Ed represents the kind of amiability that he thinks is out of place."
—LAWRENCE KASDAN

TIGHTER STILL, we return to the words "Ed Masterson murdered..."

WYATT'S FACE. Deep pain. The confirmation of so many hard truths.

EXT. FRONT STREET, DODGE CITY—NIGHT
CLOSE ON the Dodge "Dead Line" Sign being lifted from a pile of garbage. It is shot full of bullet holes. Wyatt's hands set it upright and slide it into a hole in the dirt.

UP to Wyatt's face. He turns to look at Bat, who hands him his shotgun.

Waiting for them a few feet away are Morgan, Virgil, and another deputy named SHERM McMASTERS, all heavily armed.

           WYATT
  Let's go.

The five men begin walking down the street.

INT. COMIQUE THEATRE AND SALOON—NIGHT
We're looking at the front entrance from the inside, but what we HEAR is chaos: fighting, gunfire, rowdiness. The five lawmen come quietly in the front door. As the other four move out of frame, we move in tight on Wyatt. He fires his shotgun into the ceiling. The room goes silent.

           WYATT
  My name is Wyatt Earp. It all ends now!

EXT. RESTAURANT—DAY
Wyatt, Virgil and Bat come out, lighting cigars, look around, start down the street. Bat now walks with a slight limp and uses a fancy walking stick.

           BAT
  Quiet since I got back from Texas.

           VIRGIL
  Things have slowed down a little bit.

WYATT

Hell, the other day I bought a pair of
shoes.

Wyatt sees something and stops. The others follow his look.

A buckboard wagon is pulling up toward them.
On the front seat, dusty from a journey, sits Doc
Holliday and his companion, BIG NOSE KATE.
She's a tough, robust whore with a hard-nosed,
sardonic view of the world.

WYATT

Hello, Doc.

DOC

Wyatt. I'd like you to meet my friend,
Kate Elder.

WYATT

Nice to meet you, Miss Elder.

BIG NOSE KATE

Charmed, I'm sure. You can call me Big
Nose Kate…everybody else does.

The three lawmen can't help focusing on that
particular facial feature in the midst of their
amusement.

BIG NOSE KATE
No, it ain't that big. All kinds of reasons
a person gets a name.

BAT
I couldn't agree more.

WYATT
This is my brother Virgil...Bat Masterson. Doc Holliday.

DOC
(impressed)
Bat Masterson. You're the man that
killed Sergeant King in Sweetwater?

Bat nods, not knowing Doc's feelings about the
deceased.

DOC
Got you in the leg, I understand. My
congratulations to you, sir. King was a
skunk of the first order.

BIG NOSE KATE
I wish you'd got him before he shot poor
Molly Brennan. She was a sweet girl.

This is a subject of real feeling for Bat, who
loved the dead girl. Quietly—

BAT
Yes she was, ma'am.

WYATT
What brings you to Dodge City, Doc?

DOC
I guess I missed you, Wyatt.

BIG NOSE KATE
This is where the money is.

VIRGIL
Anything else?

Doc looks at Virgil; he already likes him less
than Wyatt.

DOC
Perhaps you've heard...we had an unfortunate incident in Ft. Griffin, entirely
beyond our control. It seemed a good
time to move on.

WYATT
I hope we won't have anything unfortunate happen in Dodge.

DOC
Likewise, I'm sure. I'll be checking my
gun as soon as we find a hotel. I look forward to more civilized surroundings.

WYATT
You came to the right place.

They nod their understanding to each other
and Doc moves the wagon out.

VIRGIL
Maybe he ought to check his knife, too.
He cut the man in Texas from his belly
to his dick.

INT. COMIQUE THEATRE AND
SALOON—NIGHT
A traveling Gilbert & Sullivan troupe, the
Pauline Markham Players (the English Opera
Company) is vigorously performing "H.M.S.
Pinafore" on stage. About half the occupants of
the saloon are engrossed in the performance,
which must compete for auditory supremacy
with the hubbub of the working saloon and
gambling house.

Doc and Bat are among the players in a poker
game. Morgan is dealing Faro. Mattie is trolling
the room looking for her next john.

EXT. COMIQUE THEATRE—NIGHT
Wyatt and Virgil come up the street, making
their rounds.

VIRGIL
…don't know what you want, Wyatt.
This set-up seems pretty sweet to me.
We're makin' good money…and it looks
like we'll get a piece of the Alhambra
Faro bank—

WYATT
Virgil, there's never been a man that got
rich working on a salary, that much I've
learned.

VIRGIL
If we wanted to get rich, we went into
the wrong line of work.

WYATT
(gives him a look)
That's what I'm saying.

VIRGIL
You think it's gonna be different in
Tombstone?

WYATT

Can't say, but there's silver there. And opportunity. The town is booming. They're going to need saloons, stage lines, hotels—you name it.

COMIQUE THEATRE—NIGHT

They stop at the open doors of the Comique and survey the lively scene. Virgil laughs at Wyatt's last statement.

VIRGIL

Did it ever occur to you that maybe we're doin' the only thing we're any good at?

It definitely had occurred to him, but for Wyatt it's no laughing matter. Virgil moves on down the sidewalk, leaving Wyatt looking inside.

WYATT'S POV. His gaze travels from the poker game with Doc and Bat to Mattie, who is unaware of him as she works the room. Wyatt's look is hard, unsettled. He looks up at the stage.

WYATT'S POV. The show is in mid-performance. During an energetic dance interlude the "Cabin Boy" character moves to the front of the stage. In the midst of his "sailor's hornpipe" dance, his cap accidentally flies off. Long dark tresses unfurl around a *beautiful young woman's face*. There's a loud HOOTING reaction from the audience as the only mildly flustered Young Beauty reclaims her cap.

Wyatt has been struck by the thunderbolt. He is mesmerized. (He does not hear the approaching HOOFBEATS in the street outside.) Wyatt takes a side step to try and keep the girl in view as she moves back among the dancing performers, disappearing.

Wyatt is about to move into the theatre when the chandelier above the poker table EXPLODES, raining glass down on the players. Suddenly the roar of GUNSHOTS and WHOOPING fill the street behind Wyatt. The occupants of the theatre hit the deck (except for Doc, who is either very cool or in an alcoholic stupor) as more bullets hit inside. The Performers scurry for the wings.

Wyatt spins in the doorway. The window next to him SHATTERS from a bullet and there is a SCREAM inside as someone is hit.

In the street, six Drunken Cowboys are getting in a last "hurrah" on their way out of town. The one who just shot at Wyatt aims and fires again. The lead members of the group are already beginning to gallop out of town.

Now we see something we have not seen before: Wyatt draws like lightning, aims from his chest—takes just a fraction of a second longer than we expect—and fires. This is the pure act.

The Cowboy is blown off his horse, dead. The other Cowboys look in horror and turn tail, riding out of town, past Virgil, down the block, who fires at them without result.

Wyatt lowers his gun. There is no remorse in his eyes. There is not much of anything there. This is what he does.

Joanna Going as Josie (center).

EXT. VIRGIL'S HOUSE—DAY

Virgil and his wife, ALLIE, a feisty, hard-working waitress, are talking quietly on the porch of the tiny little house. As Wyatt comes down the street toward the house, Virgil parts from his wife and comes up the walk, where he meets Wyatt.

WYATT

What's this all about?

Virgil doesn't know. He shrugs and heads out into the street.

WYATT
Where you going?

VIRGIL
Allie says they want to talk to you alone.

Wyatt looks confused as he watches Virgil walk away. He turns and heads down the walk, where Allie waits, holding the front door.

INT. FRONT ROOM, VIRGIL'S HOUSE—DAY
The tiny room is pretty much full to the limit. Waiting for Wyatt, in various stages of discomfort, are Bessie, Mattie, and Lou. Allie leads Wyatt in and motions him to the best chair. He declines and remains standing with his hat in his hands. The women greet him quietly.

BESSIE
Thanks for comin', Wyatt. You may be wonderin' what this is.

WYATT
(quiet and flat)
You're damn right.

Mattie knows that tone; she seems about to crawl under the rug. She can't meet his gaze. Allie is uncowed.

ALLIE
We've all been talking. We like it here in Dodge.

Wyatt still doesn't get it. His look falls on young Lou, who squirms and looks away, afraid of him.

BESSIE
(a tad harsh)
…We want you to stop talkin' to our husbands about goin' to Tombstone…

ALLIE
…and all that nonsense about mining claims and starting your own businesses…

LOU
(takes all her courage)
They all listen to you, Wyatt. They'll do
what you say…I know Morgan will…

ALLIE
We want you to leave well enough alone,
and just for once let the Earps settle
down somewhere.

Wyatt gives them a long look. Hard.

WYATT
Is that right?
(emphatic agreement from the
women)
You brought me here to tell me that,
without my brothers?

The women say nothing. Wyatt shakes his
head, a slightly disgusted look on his face. Then
he turns and walks out.

INT. HOTEL—NIGHT
Several Residents of the hotel and a Desk Clerk
are gathered worriedly at the bottom of the
main stairs as Wyatt hurries in from the street.
They point him upstairs just as a GUNSHOT
sounds up there.

RESIDENT
It's that goddamn Holliday and his—

Wyatt fixes him with a withering glare that
stops him in mid-sentence. The man cowers,
shrinking back. Wyatt takes the steps three at a
time.

INT. UPSTAIRS HALLWAY—NIGHT
Wyatt quickly approaches a doorway. There's
another GUNSHOT and a hole blasts out of
the door, the wall across from it explodes and
there is a muffled SCREAM from some terrified
occupant of another room. Wyatt draws his gun
and stands to the side of the door.

*From left, Mattie,
Lou, Bessie, Allie
Earp (Catherine
O'Hara), and
Wyatt.*

"One of the things that was attractive to me about doing Wyatt Earp was the women. It's
not that the women have big parts, it's that they play a big part in the movie. In most
Earp stories the women are dismissed by the filmmakers. Our movie shows how they're
dismissed, which is very different than giving a woman a part and dismissing the part by
failing to write their feelings and their humiliations. We show how they were dismissed.
They were cut out. The brothers said, 'You can't be in this conversation. It's me and my
brothers.' And that's good for the movie. It's hard on the characters, but it's also very
enlightening. It's very original. And anyone who sees it may cringe, but they will immedi-

WYATT
Doc…Kate…it's Wyatt! I'm coming in. Don't shoot me.

Wyatt turns the knob and pushes open the door. He looks, then enters.

INT. DOC'S ROOM—NIGHT
Big Nose Kate stands at the wall opposite the door, her mouth and chin bloody, her cheek freshly bruised. She's waving a big army revolver. On the other side of the room, next to the door, Doc is on the floor, his back propped against the wall. At the moment, he's struggling to his feet and pulling a beautiful dagger (a dirk)

from his boot. He's obviously drunk, but not sloppy. He raises the dirk toward Kate, smiling that death's-head grin of his.

DOC
Come on, little dove, let's finally get it over with…

BIG NOSE KATE
Don't think I won't, you skinny heap of pus! I won't have you hit me ever again.

Wyatt has no trouble reaching over and taking the dirk from Doc's hand; the dentist seems barely aware of Wyatt until he does. Wyatt eyes Kate.

WYATT
Put that gun down, Kate. I don't want you killing me by mistake.

BIG NOSE KATE
…Year after year, sleepin' in his bed, breathin' the diseased air he coughs up all night…no one else would come near him…
    (wipes blood from her mouth)
…And this is what I get…this is his idea of a fair hand.

WYATT
    (soothing)
You won't be shooting him tonight, Kate.

DOC
Let her do it. They can hang the bitch and we'll both be happy—

Wyatt pulls back quickly and punches Doc hard across the jaw. He goes down hard, out.

EXT. HORSE TROUGH, SECOND AVENUE—NIGHT
Wyatt pulls Doc out of the water, having dunked him a few times already. Surprisingly, when he gets his breath and stops coughing, Doc is laughing; from Doc the sound is a disconcerting rattle. Wyatt lowers him to the ground, propped against the trough. Wyatt settles on the edge of the trough, idly shaking off the water he's accumulated.

WYATT
What's wrong with you?

This causes Doc to laugh and choke again.

>DOC
>"What's wrong with me?" What have you got?
>(he laughs again)
>I'm dyin' of tuberculosis, everyone who knows me hates me, I sleep with the nastiest whore in Kansas and...every morning I wake up surprised...surprised I have to spend another day in this pisshole world.

Wyatt regards him with an odd affection.

>WYATT
>Not everybody that knows you hates you.

Doc accepts that gratefully, without looking at him. Doc looks disdainfully across the street at a small group of people staring at them.

>WYATT
>What were you fighting about this time?

>DOC
>(thinks, shrugs)
>Can't remember. But, like most times when Kate and I disagree, we set to killing each other.

Doc looks up to see Wyatt gazing at the people watching them. Doc can no longer contain himself; he leans toward them and shouts—

>DOC
>All of you can kiss my skinny ass!

The people disperse. Wyatt gives Doc a look.

>WYATT
>Doc, sometimes I think being your friend is more trouble than it's worth.

>DOC
>Maybe...but I'll be there when you need me.

Doc is looking off into the night as he says this. Wyatt looks down at him. He knows it's true.

EXT. CEMETERY OUTSIDE DODGE
CITY—DAY
Bat and Wyatt stand once more over Ed's gravestone. In the background, Doc can be seen heading toward them with a bottle in hand.

>WYATT
>People liked Ed.

>BAT
>Yep. They say it was the biggest funeral in the history of Dodge. 'Course the town ain't that old.

Wyatt looks at Bat a long moment.

>BAT
>We've covered some ground, haven't we?

Wyatt nods. Bat knows something's up.

81

BAT
What is it?

WYATT
I've had it with bein' a lawman, Bat. I've had enough of bein' famous. I'm sick of Dodge and the whole state of Kansas.

DOC
(arriving)
What are you two doing? Can't you boys wait to get in here?

WYATT
(looks at Ed's grave)
Sayin' goodbye.

Doc acknowledges it, embarrassed.

WYATT
I'm leavin' Dodge, Doc.

DOC
Hallelujah to that.
(offers bottle)
Should we drink to it?

WYATT
I'm gonna settle down…start some kind of business where nobody wants to shoot at me anymore. My brothers and I are goin'. You're both welcome to come along.

BAT
Where's that?

WYATT
Tombstone, Arizona.

DOC
Tombstone, eh? Well, it does sound quiet, I'll give you that…

FADE TO BLACK.

REHEARSING WYATT EARP

You know, rehearsal has been many different things for me, over the years. I'm a great believer in rehearsal. But I've had a lot of different thoughts about what it can be and what it should be. Finally I realized that I don't know what rehearsal is going to be. You never do. And I've gotten comfortable with that.

"When I hear the first reading, I always feel, 'Well, we don't need to rehearse.' The actors are always so good and I'm so excited to hear the lines read. I say, 'Well, let's go. Let's shoot.' But what happens is that as you spend more time with it and start to take it apart, it does get richer. It does get better. You discover things that none of us thought were there.

"I've had a completely different experience with each rehearsal. Some of them have ended with a feeling of closure, satisfaction, completion—like we'd worked it through. What you hope is that at the end of the rehearsal, somehow, the coming apart that happens in the middle has come back together. What I realized is that you can't be guaranteed of that. And just as I've had rehearsals end that way, I've had rehearsals end with uproar, upset, people not knowing how they feel. And that turned out to be great, just as great as the other thing. Everybody goes away for a while and you don't shoot the scene for a month or three months, and your ideas about it have changed anyway. My ideas about it have changed while you're gone. And the situation on the day, the way you woke up that morning, the way I woke up, and the way the light is, and the way the trucks are stuck in the mud, all those things affect what we do that day anyway.

"So we're not trying to arrive at any kind of completion. I don't want to nail anything down. What I want to do is have a conversation about what kind of movie we're making. A big part of that conversation is reading the script, hearing these words, hearing all these voices in concert. And that's a very exciting thing for me because it's why you're all here—because I love the sound of your voices and I'm dying to hear what your voices sound like in conjunction with these other people."

—FROM KASDAN'S OPENING COMMENTS TO THE CAST ON THE FIRST DAY OF REHEARSAL

That rehearsal week was really unusual for me. I hadn't had an experience like that where an entire cast was kept in the same room watching each other try to figure out [their parts], with [the director] encouraging us to struggle, to be brave and try new things.

"Rehearsals are for the director. I don't believe they are for the actors. We're supposed to get as much as we can, but they're for Larry and he was so clear that first day. And I remember feeling, and other actors feeling, like maybe it would be more comfortable in smaller groups. But Larry said, 'This is how it's going to be and this is how it's going to best serve. You will get something, Mare, you watching the Earp brothers, you're going to get something.' 'Catherine? You and Annabeth, you're going to watch Josie and Wyatt's stuff and you're going to get something.' And he was really right. All the questions that the other actors had, fed into questions of my own.

"That rehearsal was the most unusual rehearsal period I've ever had and the most rewarding for long-term, feed the tree, feed the whole organism kind of thing. It was wonderful."

—MARE WINNINGHAM (MATTIE)

We had a long rehearsal process. It was fairly intense, and I learned a lot during that process. It was a tough week of ripping up and tearing down, and everybody trying to find who their characters were. It's important, I realize now, to have had that.

"Larry, reputation-wise, for years has been an actor's director. He's a guy who makes his needs known and what his expectations are from you as an actor and from you as an actor as this character. I've never had the luxury of having a rehearsal process where you spend six days, twelve hours a day, in a room with a bunch of other actors, going over a script that does not change. This script was in such good shape, as I assume it always is with Larry, that you just work on the material at hand. That's a tremendous advantage. I mean, I've been in a lot of movies where they talk about rehearsal periods, but I've never done this, never had the chance to do this. Now

the question is, you get used to doing this, what are you gonna do next time, when you don't have the chance? But I'd love it if this was the way it was done all the time."

—MARK HARMON (JOHNNY BEHAN)

That rehearsal was such a crazy week. It was a very intense week, I think, for so many people. I think people wanted an answer. People wanted to come out of the rehearsal and go, 'Okay. Now I know what I'm supposed to do.' And Larry just kind of kept it as a continuously open and unfolding process. Larry wasn't showing his hand. He was kind of sitting over there kind of poker-faced, going, 'I want you to do it again,' and I think that created an anxiety in a lot of the actors because they wanted to know they were on the right track or something. But the flip side is that I think it really instilled the sense that nothing's written in stone here, so that when we came to the actual day of shooting, we were still in the process of finding it, as opposed to just trying to recreate something we've already done. It established the ongoing sense that it was a continual evolution of characters."

—DAVID ANDREWS (JAMES)

I think what rehearsals did for me and what they did for everybody was to make clear that nothing was written in stone about how something would be played or how it wouldn't be played, but we were all on the same path. We were all thinking alike or similarly. We were all kind of in the same groove."

—LINDEN ASHBY (MORGAN)

People have different work habits. Rehearsal forced everybody to concentrate for five days in a row. It also allowed Larry and me to see what people's patterns were and maybe anticipate trouble. I mean, I was going to act with every one of those people, so I got a chance to hear them talk and see how they would move and what they would do. You see what people's strengths are."

—KEVIN COSTNER

CHAPTER THREE

"Show us an honest cowboy."

FADE IN:

A sign—"Welcome to TOMBSTONE, ARIZONA. No carrying of Firearms within the City Limits."

EXT. VIRGIL'S HOUSE, TOMBSTONE, ARIZONA (1881)–DAY
A twelve-year–old Barboy struggles along balancing the weight of two large buckets of beer, as he passes the sign. He approaches the small, plain house and wobbles down the side.

EXT. BACKYARD, VIRGIL'S HOUSE—DAY
The Barboy brings the beer into the diminutive backyard, crowded now with Earps, here for a family gathering. The "wives"—Bessie, Mattie, Lou and Allie—move in and out of the house carrying food and dishes to one of two tables that have been set up out here. At the other table, the brothers—Wyatt, Virgil, Morgan, and James—are gathered around a ledger and various financial papers. The Barboy deposits the beer with the food and James flips him a coin before he leaves. Lou comes over and puts her arms around Morgan affectionately.

LOU
Morg honey, supper's ready. Come on, sweetie.

MORGAN
Be right there, Lou darlin'.

BESSIE
(sees this, can't stand it)
I'm gonna be sick.

MATTIE
(sharply)
Wyatt, the food's on the table.

WYATT
(gives her a look)
Good, Mattie. That way we'll know where to find it when we're finished.
(back to the ledger)
...In mining claims we have the Mountain Maid Mine, the Grasshopper, the Earp, the Dodge, and the Mattie Blaylock.

LOU
Morg honey, how come you never named a mine after me?

BESSIE
(a rough customer)
They will, Lou honey. They'll call the next one The Idiot.

MORGAN
Damn it, Bessie!

JAMES
Bessie, shut up and have a drink.

VIRGIL
Go ahead, Wyatt.

WYATT
We're about fifty-fifty between mines that are producing and mines that are—

ALLIE
—worthless.

WYATT
...that are not producing.

JAMES
In other words, we ain't seen a dime's profit from the lot of 'em.

BESSIE
Not in other words, James...those are the words.

WYATT
Income...we got our salaries, James's Sampling Room, plus half interest in the Oriental Faro bank and quarter interest in one at the Crystal Palace.

MORGAN
(laughs)
Hell, from the sound of it you'd think we'd have some money by now.

VIRGIL
I'm afraid we're about as rich as lawmen are ever gonna be...'cause when you get through all the talk, that's what we are.

"WE'RE YOUR WIVES."

Women were different in the 1800s. They were living in different circumstances. It's a very interesting type of womanhood to play because it is set against the background of the new frontier, and the new West, and the unsureness of it all. I think that most women, if they really wanted to establish a family and a home life and some sort of security, had to be very focused and very clear. They had to strive for order in their own lives against the background of the chaos of the time.

"Maybe there aren't a lot of books about frontier women because they were not the most celebrated heroes or heroines. But they're the silent sort of heroines, heroines truly because they were stable, rooted, hard-working women. They were the survivors, and they took care of the men, and they took care of the children, and they took care of the food. I think that's one of the things that separates this movie from being a typical western, per se, because it's not just about the men. It's also about the women who changed the men's feelings and who colored the way that they looked at the world."

—ANNABETH GISH (URILLA)

You can tell a lot about the women of this period from the way they dressed and the way they did their hair. It was all so complicated. I mean, they were out here in the Wild West and it was smelly and dirty and there was dust everywhere. And yet they were walking around in Victorian costume, in the most gussied-up buttons and bows and frills. They just clung to that tradition even though they were out here in these little cowtowns, these mining camps. I think that really reveals something about their spirit, and their desire to maintain culture."

—JOANNA GOING (JOSIE)

None of the books about the Earps gave me much insight into the working world [*the world of prostitutes*] but I knew that there are books on prostitutes and I found one. As opportunities went for women in that time... the idea of having power in the world was appealing. That's what makes the world go around. I don't think it's crazy to have seen prostitution as a way to get power, because it allowed some sort of economic freedom. I thought that was worth thinking about. And that's not to say that it isn't a mind-blower to end up underneath somebody in order to make money. I'd never want to undercut the fact that this does have repercussions on the psyche. But if you're bartering and you're using your body to barter, and you're living in a time when you have absolutely no power and when you're not even aware that there's a struggle for power because it's not even an opportunity to exploit, then the idea of making some money would be rather alluring. And I believe that those women who went out there and did that were a breed apart. They set themselves apart just by doing that."

—MARE WINNINGHAM (MATTIE)

I don't think these women represent the average woman of that time. They were like gypsies, they traveled a lot, their husbands led these mysterious lives that they didn't really let the wives in on (unless they had to because there was a body in the house or something). They were men who looked for trouble, only they were men of the law, and not outlaws...

"Also, there's not a lot of hope for these characters, the wives. They're disregarded pretty completely—victimized, in a way, by these men, who value each other above anything else. From my point of view, I think of the Earp brothers as a sort of gang, and that wasn't such a great thing for the women in their lives."

—CATHERINE O'HARA (ALLIE)

I think the women definitely had to be as tough as the men. To be a single woman in those times almost always meant you were a prostitute because there was really no other way to make a living for yourself unless you were hooked up with a man. So these women were very tough. They were survivors. That's how they got out there, and that's how they survived being out there....

"I think many of the women were probably leaving pretty rough situations behind. You know, maybe farms or families that were abusive, or they ran off with a man and he left her, this sort of thing. Women didn't tend to come out to these parts on their own, in most cases, unless for some reason they had to. There just weren't that many opportunities for women on the frontier."

—JOBETH WILLIAMS (BESSIE)

"In 1879 Dodge City was beginning to lose much of the snap which had given it a charm to men of restless blood, and I decided to move to Tombstone, which was just building up a reputation. Doc Holliday thought he would move with me . . . I was tired of the trials of a peace officer's life and wanted no more of it. But as luck would have it, I stopped at Prescott, Arizona, to see my brother Virgil and while there I met C.P. Dake, the United States Marshal of the Territory. Dake had heard of me before, and he begged me so hard to take the deputyship in Tombstone that I finally consented. It was thus that the real troubles of a lifetime began."   —WYATT EARP

Wyatt shoots him a quick, hard look. He's irritable about Virgil's continuing refrain.

                    ALLIE
That's good enough for me, sweetheart. I
married you for your looks.

                    BESSIE
I guess you lost out all around.

Virgil just laughs; he reaches out to grab Allie, but she eludes him, throws him a wink. Wyatt goes back to the ledger.

                    WYATT
We have close to fourteen thousand dollars in liquidity.

This brings Bessie over to the men's table for the first time.

                    BESSIE
Why don't we just split it up and everybody do what they like?

                    WYATT
          (going on)
What we've got to decide is how to
invest it.

                    BESSIE
Don't you ignore me, Wyatt! If somebody voted you king of this family I didn't hear about it. You drag us all down here with a lotta talk about ownin' businesses and gettin' rich…and here you are a year later a bunch of lawmen and bartenders just like before.

                    JAMES
Bessie…you know some things haven't worked out like we'd like. That's nobody's fault.

The other wives have stopped their bustling preparations. They stop and watch.

                    VIRGIL
We didn't all come out here to split up
stakes.

                    MORGAN
We're tryin' to stick together and build
something.

                    BESSIE
Why? Why's it always got to be the brothers…the brothers together? James… why can't it just be you and me?

She looks at the other women.

                    BESSIE
They're afraid to say it but they think the same as me. We're your wives. Don't we ever count more than the damn brothers?

                    WYATT
No, Bessie…you don't.

There is a hard silence. Wyatt speaks very quietly—

                    WYATT
Wives come and go…That's the plain truth of it. They run off…
          (he looks down)
…they die.

Mattie averts her eyes, which fill with tears. She turns and goes into the house. Allie watches her.

                    ALLIE
You're a cold man, Wyatt…God forgive you, you are cold.

INT. WYATT'S ROOMS—NIGHT
Mattie lies under the covers, staring at the ceiling. Wyatt wearily takes off his shirt, then stops undressing and sits on the edge of the bed.

                    WYATT
I'm sorry if I hurt you today. That was not my intention.

She turns to him with sudden urgency.

                    MATTIE
Let's have children, Wyatt.

                    WYATT
Mattie …

                    MATTIE
You're always talkin' about family…then let's have children, a family of our own. Our children, Wyatt, yours and mine… before I'm too old for it, before I dry up inside. I can feel it, Wyatt, part of me is starting to die. But it's not too late.

90

Wyatt looks at her a long moment.

> WYATT
> Children aren't a part of the bargain, Mattie. They never were.

Mattie's face crumbles. She turns away as she begins to cry.

EXT. CHINATOWN—DAY
Tombstone's thriving Chinatown (Hoptown), with its exotic joss houses, laundries and herb stores. Chinese in traditional dress with long pigtails and caps squat over coal stoves, preparing pungent smelling meats; dumpling dough hangs like laundry and the residents create a cacophony of warring dialects. Two Young Men are whitewashing the side of a building on which has been crudely painted the slogans CHINKS GO BACK TO CHINA and JOHN CHINAMAN MUST GO!

Sitting in a big chair on the porch of her restaurant smoking a long pipe is CHINA MARY, an immense older woman, who is the most powerful person in Hoptown. She looks up sharply and takes in this sight—

A dust-covered, dog-tired Group passes by on horseback: a returning Posse made up of Wyatt, Morgan, and MARSHAL FRED WHITE, and their two Prisoners, hands tied to the saddlehorns of their horses, FRANK STILLWELL and PETE SPENCE.

EXT. FREMONT STREET—DAY
They have turned onto this busy, commercial thoroughfare and are attracting excited attention from the Locals as they ride past Fly's Boarding House and Photo Gallery and pull up down the block in front of the Merchandise Exchange, a cluster of three buildings contain-

TRANSFORMING DODGE CITY, KANSAS, INTO TOMBSTONE, ARIZONA

Because Dodge and Tombstone were the two largest towns and had to be shot at the same location, this was the most important change of looks—and the most difficult. So the question is, 'How do we take the same street and change it over, to look like another street?' You make very specific decisions—'This is how it's going to look when we start, this is how it's going to look changed over.'

"The biggest difference, and it was in the research, was that Tombstone at that time was mostly single story buildings with a lot of porches—high porches. Basically that's what I held to in Tombstone. Dodge is a much bigger city, an established cattle town. I put a second story on the buildings and took the porches off. You can change the sense of a street by changing the shape of it, putting another corner on it.

"It's just a trick. It's easy to change things around and trick the audience, because they have no point of reference. If you change colors or you change the details, it looks like a different place."

—IDA RANDOM

We keyed off of the historical differences. Tombstone was much more a desert town. Dodge City was a plains town, cattle town. And since we were doing both towns in exactly the same location, we had to use the differences in the facades to help us. We tried to reshape the streets so that one was not identifiable as the other. We had to be very careful about the surrounding scenery. Since the bulk of the work was in Tombstone, I decided to use the surrounding terrain freely [while shooting that sequence]. In Dodge City we will never look out at those mountains. We will never see that horizon that we freely see in Tombstone. Ida did an incredible job with the change-over. I could barely tell what used to be what, and I know the place pretty well."

—LAWRENCE KASDAN

ing the county offices and courtrooms. A Crowd gathers around the group. Pushing his way through the crowd is the editor of the *Tombstone Epitaph*, JOHN P. CLUM.

INT. COURTROOM—DAY
The two prisoners are standing before the bench of JUDGE WELLS SPICER. Both men look the worse for wear, and Stillwell has sus-

tained a pistol-whipping that's left his head bandaged and bruised.

JUDGE SPICER
…that you, Frank Stillwell, and you, Pete Spence, did on the evening of September 8, 1881, rob the Sandy Bob stagecoach on the road from Tombstone to Bisbee. How do you plead?

STILLWELL
Not guilty...and that's not all I got to
say—

JUDGE SPICER
You'll get your chance. Spence?

SPENCE
I didn't do nothin', Judge. It's all a set-up
job by those damn Earps and Marshal
White!

STILLWELL
(showing his injuries)
Look at me, Judge! This is how they treat
you when you come nice and easy-like to
defend your good name.

Wyatt and Fred White are impassive. Morgan
reacts, grinning, and—

MORGAN
Nice and easy, my ass...

JUDGE SPICER
Quiet, all of you! There's enough evidence and eyewitnesses to warrant an
indictment. Bail is set at...$7000 each.
Have you the means?

IKE CLANTON
They got it!

There is movement at the back of the room as a
rough group of Cowboys make their arrival
known. In the group: IKE CLANTON, his
young brother BILLY CLANTON, FRANK
McLAURY and his younger brother TOM
McLAURY, and a handsome, dangerous-looking fellow named CURLY BILL BROCIUS.
The assembled Locals give them a wide berth;
only Ike comes forward, passing John Clum,
who's seated in the courtroom now. Ike exchanges a poisonous look with the three
lawmen.

IKE CLANTON
We'll stand the money, Judge. And get
'em away from these bastards before they
find themselves lynched.

FRANK McLAURY
(from the back)
There's not an honest cowboy that can
get a fair shake in this town!

MORGAN
First show us an honest cowboy!

This causes a stir in the crowd. There's a lot of
hostility toward the Cowboys.

JUDGE SPICER
That's enough! The next man who
speaks will be fined $25 for contempt of
court.

CURLY BILL
(yells from back)
Your Honor, $25 wouldn't pay for half the contempt I got for this court.

The Judge slams down his gavel.

JUDGE SPICER
Bailiff, collect $50 from Curly Bill Brocius.

EXT. MERCHANDISE EXCHANGE—DAY
The Cowboys, led by Ike, mount up to head out of town. Wyatt, Morgan, Marshal White, and John Clum watch from the sidewalk. Virgil walks up to join them; he also wears a badge.

VIRGIL
Didn't take 'em long to get back on the road.

CLUM
Clanton paid their bail. That's the law, and it's the same for them as it is for you or me.

WYATT
Then I guess it don't work too well.

DOWN THE STREET. As the Cowboys move along, they pass a Second Posse coming into town, this one much more friendly. It is led by COUNTY SHERIFF JOHNNY BEHAN. He gives Ike a questioning look.

BEHAN
What happened, Ike?

IKE CLANTON
(irritated)
You're a little late, Johnny.

He spurs his horse and leads the Cowboys out. Several greet Johnny, who then turns in at the Merchandise Exchange and dismounts. Irritated, he speaks to Marshal White.

BEHAN
What's wrong with you, Fred? Why didn't you send word when you caught up with them in Bisbee?

MARSHAL WHITE
Didn't know where to find you, Johnny.

BEHAN
I'm the County Sheriff…those men were caught in my jurisdiction! I should have been at the hearing.

WYATT
They had enough friends there, as it was.

BEHAN
(defensive)
We've been all over hell looking for those two.

WYATT
Maybe you weren't looking hard enough, Behan.

Wyatt turns and walks away.

MORGAN
All over hell? That sounds like your jurisdiction all right.

EXT. BAKERY/ SIDEWALK, FOURTH STREET—DAY
Wyatt and Virgil amble down the sidewalk in the morning light. Wyatt stops at the open door of a bakery and looks inside, part of a ritual.

WYATT
Good morning, Maria.

MARIA (OS)
Buenos dias, Mr. Wyatt!

With that, a hot, freshly baked roll comes flying out the door into Wyatt's hand. He nods his gratitude and follows Virgil, juggling the hot roll until it's cool enough to bite. GEORGE SPANGENBERG is sweeping the sidewalk in front of his Gun Shop. He chuckles as the Earps approach, nodding at something across the street. They look over there.

Johnny Behan is checking his hair and spiffy outfit in the window of the Wells Fargo Office.

SPANGENBERG
Look at Behan. I think he'd lick himself all over if he could, he's so whipped-up.

VIRGIL
What's with him?

Wyatt munches distractedly on the roll.

SPANGENBERG
His woman's comin' back from San Francisco on the Prescott stage…the Jewish girl.

WYATT
I never knew him to have one woman.

VIRGIL
(gives Wyatt a funny look)
I guess you haven't seen her.

SPANGENBERG
Oh, he's been busy while she was gone, but I reckon he'll stay home tonight.

The Wells Fargo stagecoach comes around the corner and pulls up in front of the depot. Johnny hops around, looking inside, then hurries around to open the streetside door and help down his lady. She's wearing a big bonnet that hides her face at first, but as she steps onto the street, she is revealed—

This is the very Young Beauty whom Wyatt saw for a moment on the stage of the Comique Theatre in Dodge City, dancing the "sailor's hornpipe" as the Cabin Boy. She's a Jewess, barely twenty, and her name is JOSEPHINE SARAH MARCUS—JOSIE to her friends. Wyatt reacts with the same dumbstruck force as in Dodge City.

Behan sweeps her into his arms and gives her a passionate kiss, more passionate perhaps than she would prefer in this setting. When he finally releases her and turns away to collect her bags, Josie's face is flushed. She straightens her bonnet and then looks up, her gaze crossing the street and lighting (and that's the word) on Wyatt. She gives him a long, fearless look, straight into him, then turns away.

Virgil looks over at Wyatt and laughs out loud. Wyatt, caught, takes a bite from the roll and turns to walk down the sidewalk ahead of Virgil.

INT. ORIENTAL SALOON—NIGHT
A beautiful, elaborate saloon with an endless, ornate bar, worth a fortune. The place is busy almost any time it's dark outside. The Earps have a partial interest in the gambling here and at any time you're likely to find one of them or one of their friends running a Faro bank. Tonight, Doc Holliday is behind one table (he's followed

Wyatt from Dodge) and Wyatt himself is running another.

Morgan moves in to replace Wyatt behind the table. He indicates Johnny Behan at the bar watching them—

> MORGAN
> The outlaw's best friend would like a word with you.

Wyatt gives a dour look, but gives his place up to Morgan and moves out.

AT AN UNOCCUPIED TABLE in the corner, Wyatt slides into a chair with a cup of coffee, while Behan sits down with a bottle of whiskey and two shot glasses, both of which he fills. He slides one toward Wyatt, who shakes his head, declining.

> BEHAN
> Just tonight, maybe…to peace?

> WYATT
> No exceptions.

> BEHAN
> (friendly)
> That about sums you up, doesn't it, Wyatt…no exceptions.

> WYATT
> What's on your mind?

> BEHAN
> You're headed for a war with Ike Clanton and the men he rides with. And it's all over nothing. You and Ike want the same things, the same things we all want.

> WYATT
> Really?

> BEHAN
> That's right…to prosper, to have some security for our families. Wyatt, you didn't come to Tombstone to be a lawman again. You're an entrepreneur. You're full of ideas for making the Earps rich.
> (studies Wyatt, can't tell how he's doing)
> Nothing good can come from you interfering with the business of the Clantons and the McLaurys…only blood. But with a little cooperation, everyone can make out.

> WYATT
> How's that?

> BEHAN
> (leans in confidentially)
> Money, Wyatt, lots of it…to be shared with everyone who helps. I know you, Wyatt. That's what you've always been after.

WYATT

I think you've forgotten something. The Clantons and their friends are rustlers.

BEHAN

What does it matter to you if they're running Mexican cattle up from the border? They don't tell you how to run your Faro game.

WYATT

You didn't let me finish…They're murderers and thieves. They rob the stagecoaches my brothers and I are paid to protect. One of those bastards shot old Bud Philpot, who never did a thing to anyone but drive a stage like the man he was.

BEHAN
(gives him a sharp look)
Wyatt, your best friend is the worst killer in the territory. Some people say Doc was in on that robbery that got Bud killed. Even Big Nose Kate said it—

WYATT

That was *your work*, Johnny—you got her drunk and mad to say that.
(he stands up)
I'm sick of hearing your lies. Go back to your friends. Tell them if they want to make a fight with the Earps, they know where to find us.

Wyatt walks away.

Over at his faro bank, Doc Holliday has been watching.

EXT. FRONT STREET—MORNING
Wyatt crosses the street, busy with morning activity. He's just reached the sidewalk when Doc comes out of the Campbell & Hatch Saloon. He looks bad. The two men move down the street.

WYATT

You look like shit.

DOC

Good morning to you, too, sir.

WYATT

Ever thought about getting some sleep at night?

DOC

Can't get settled 'til the sun comes up.

Ike Clanton and Frank McLaury exit the Oriental Saloon, squinting their hangovers against the sun. They pause on their way to the hitching posts, looking around. Suddenly, like everyone else in the vicinity, they hear—

SADDLE TRAMP (OS)

Wyatt Earp!

Wyatt and Doc turn to the sound of the voice. Standing in the middle of the street is a dangerous-looking SADDLE TRAMP, a man with a scarred face who wears his holster low-slung and looks as if he knows how to use it.

SADDLE TRAMP

Wyatt Earp, I been waiting all night in this stinkin' town for you to show yer yella face!

The street takes on a certain hush, with innocents scurrying to get out of the way. Doc lifts his hand in a peaceful gesture and takes one step toward the Saddle Tramp.

DOC

Now listen, mister, if you've got a problem with my friend—

Randall Mell as John Clum

"The situation in Tombstone was aggravated by the general feeling among the citizens that the peace officers of the county under Sheriff John Behan were in sympathy with the lawless element which roamed southeastern Arizona and it was deemed wise to guard against possible depredations of these outlaws. Our plans for law enforcement and protection of our lives and property were fully and freely discussed with Wyatt Earp and his brother Virgil. This fact establishes beyond any question the high esteem and confidence which the leading citizens of Tombstone entertained toward both Wyatt and Virgil."

—JOHN P. CLUM, EDITOR OF THE TOMBSTONE EPITAPH

The Saddle Tramp raises his left hand and points at Doc.

> SADDLE TRAMP
> One more step!
> (Doc stops)
> I got no quarrel with you, but I ain't picky.

Doc begins to square up against him, a devilish smile piercing his face.

> DOC
> Well, no one ever accused me of bein' picky either, so why don't we just —

> WYATT
> Doc.

The message is clear in Wyatt's tone: Get out of the way. Reluctantly, Doc gives up. He looks over at Wyatt, who has thus far not moved. Doc gives a resigned shake to his head and steps back, with this to the Saddle Tramp—

> DOC
> It's your funeral, friend.

Ike and Frank exchange a look of pleased anticipation.

Now Wyatt steps forward slowly from among the horses. He stops twenty feet from the Saddle Tramp. There is a kind of gentleness in his voice when he speaks—

> WYATT
> Why are you making this terrible mistake?

> SADDLE TRAMP
> This is no mistake, you piece of dung. You shot my cousin dead in Dodge City.

> WYATT
> Your *cousin*? You're ready to die for a cousin?

The Saddle Tramp looks hard. But for the first time, there is a glimmer of doubt in his eyes.

> SADDLE TRAMP
> A stupid cowboy havin' some fun… against the great Wyatt Earp. He didn't have a chance. But, mister, I ain't no cowboy.

> WYATT
> Was he with the Pierce Cattle Crew?

The Saddle Tramp gives a tight nod.

> WYATT
> Then I can tell you he had every chance… to leave Dodge in peace. You got the same opportunity right now. But I'll also tell you, if you say one more word to degrade me…you are presently enjoying the last moments of your life.

The Saddle Tramp says nothing. He moves the fingers of his gun hand tentatively. He stares at Wyatt. *And then he wets his dry lips with his tongue.*

Doc sees it. And knows what it means. Wyatt sees it. And relaxes. It's all over. The Saddle Tramp seems to crumble from within. He takes a step backward, then another. Then he turns and runs to his horse across the street. He mounts up and rides swiftly out of town. Wyatt and Doc continue on their way. They don't even exchange a look.

Ike and Frank do. They're impressed.

EXT. ALLEN STREET—NIGHT
Wyatt rounds the corner and almost runs into Josie, coming the other way, alone.

> WYATT
> Evening, Miss.

> JOSIE
> Good evening.

She starts to move on. He hesitates, then speaks, stopping her.

> WYATT
> Are you taking a walk?

> JOSIE
> (a quizzical look)
> I am. Is that a problem?

> WYATT
> It could be in this town. A young woman walking alone at night…people could get the wrong impression.

> JOSIE
> What impression would that be? As far as I know, the red-light district is the other end of town.

WYATT

I didn't mean that. It's just that you should have an escort.

JOSIE

Mr. Earp, I can either be a shut-in or walk alone on the streets of Tombstone.

WYATT

Where's Johnny?

JOSIE

I don't know that that's any of your affair. But it happens that my fiancé's business often requires he be out at night.
(softens slightly)
But I do appreciate your concern.

Josie slowly turns to walk away. Wyatt's voice stops her.

WYATT

I saw you once before…before you came to Tombstone. In Dodge City. You were in a show…

JOSIE

I know. I saw you too. I saw you…and then you killed a man.

She turns and walks away.

INT. WYATT'S ROOMS—NIGHT
CLOSE ON Wyatt's face. He's lying in bed, staring at the ceiling. We hear light SNOR-ING. Camera MOVES UP to reveal Mattie sleeping next to Wyatt, dead to the world. Wyatt looks over at her.

INT. CAMPBELL AND HATCH SALOON AND BILLIARD PARLOR—DAY
Late afternoon. There are a few men playing pool, but the most activity is centered around Johnny Behan, who is holding court at the bar surrounded by three SALOON REGULARS. They're passing something along the bar and examining it with great interest.

BEHAN

…so I say, "What are you afraid of, dar-lin'? You're not some red Injun that thinks the camera is going to steal your soul." And she says, "No, Johnny, I'm afraid someone else might see it." But I assured her that would *never* happen.

This last pronouncement causes general LAUGHTER in the group. At that moment, Wyatt comes in and goes up to the bar to speak to the proprietor, BOB HATCH. This brings him close to Behan's group. Several of the Regulars greet Wyatt amiably. Behan and Wyatt exchange chilly looks.

> WYATT
> Bob, you seen James around?

> BOB HATCH
> Not lately.

> REGULAR #1
> Wyatt, you gotta take a look at this.

> BEHAN
> (watching Wyatt coolly)
> Now, Danny, I'm sure Marshal Earp is too upstanding, righteous…
> and married…
> (said as if it's some kind of joke)
> …to be interested in a picture of a naked young Jewish woman.

The Regular has thrust the photo forward to Wyatt just as Behan speaks. There is a split-second when Wyatt could simply choose not to look down at it. His eyes are locked on Behan's. But Wyatt cannot resist. When he looks up again, there is fire in his eyes.

> WYATT
> You're a damned fool, Behan.

> BEHAN
> Maybe, but I'm the fool that climbs into bed with that every night.

Wyatt turns and heads out.

> REGULAR #1
> What's she doing with you, Johnny?

> BEHAN
> About anything I can think of. How much detail do you want?

The Regulars laugh and Behan joins in, his eyes never leaving Wyatt's back. Wyatt leaves the saloon.

"THE CLANTONS AND THEIR FRIENDS ARE RUSTLERS. THEY'RE MURDERERS AND THIEVES."

"The cowboys numbered at one time nearly 200 but during the last two years about fifty of them have been killed. The most of them are what we call 'saddlers,' living almost wholly in the saddle and largely engaged in raiding into Sonora and adjacent country and stealing cattle, which they sell in Tombstone. It is rarely that any of these stolen cattle are recovered. When the thieves are closely pursued and it seems likely that they will be overhauled and the stock recovered, the cowboys sell the cattle to some of the butchers practically in partnership with them, and I know of cases where the finest cattle in the country have been sold at a dollar a head. When cattle are not handy the cowboys rob stages and engage in similar enterprises to raise money. As soon as they are in funds they ride into town, drink, gamble and fight. They spend their money as free as water in the saloons, dancehouses or faro banks, and this is one reason they have so many friends in town. All that large class of degraded characters who gather the crumbs of such carouses stand ready to assist them out of any trouble or into any paying rascality. The saloons and gambling houses, into whose treasuries most of the money is ultimately turned, receive them cordially and must be called warm friends of the cowboys. A good many of the merchants fear to express themselves against the criminal element because they want to keep the patronage of the cowboys friends, and the result is that when any conflict between the officers and cattle thieves or stage robbers occurs, followed up by shooting around town, as witnessed during the last few months, most of the expression of opinion comes from the desperado class and their friends, and the men who should speak loudest and most decisively to correct the condition of affairs are generally the quietest. An officer doing his duty must rely almost entirely upon his own conscience for encouragement. The sympathy of the respectable portion of the community may be with him but it is not openly expressed." —VIRGIL EARP

I play a guy named John Harris Behan, who was sheriff of Tombstone, a pretty enviable job in 1880, partially because he was sheriff which was an elected office, and also because as sheriff, he was tax collector and was able to keep a percentage of the taxes he collected. That went with the job, so it was a job that people wanted. Wyatt Earp wanted that job. Wyatt Earp also wanted John Behan's fiancée, and that's part of the story. Behan was obviously an adversary of Wyatt Earp.

"They were both lawmen, but they definitely had different ways of doing things. Wyatt Earp was a Republican, Behan was a Democrat. John Behan was much more likely to try to talk someone into giving up their gun and Wyatt Earp was much more likely to whack them on the side of the head. Two different ways of doing it. Both were respected differently in towns like this. Who's right and who's wrong?

"Behan preferred trying to align himself equally between both factions, the cowboys and the ranchers who had been here long before this boom town ever existed, and the people who came with the boom town. Because of that, he came up on both sides of the law. It also had something to do with his job. As sheriff, as tax collector, it was important for him to align himself with everybody.

"You know, I'm playing a certain character, so I find ways as an actor to find truthfulness in the actions of my character. So my tendency in playing a guy like this—I mean, I guess in terms of this script you'd say he's a bad guy, but bad guys don't think they're bad guys. I'd like to think that John Behan was really smart and that he didn't want to draw a gun against Wyatt Earp because he was smarter than that. And in some historical accounts, depending on what book you read and what opinion you have, you'll find that John Behan was thought of as very honorable and very trustworthy.

"During the rehearsal process Larry went around the room and asked, 'What's most important to each character?' When they got to me, I said, 'Himself. That's what's the most important. Johnny Behan. Himself. Self-preservation.' Nothing wrong with that, it's just his way of doing it." —MARK HARMON (JOHNNY BEHAN)

I think we want to see the villain and the hero, which Westerns have always had. And I think the audience wants to see that. They need heroes and good villains. I think a hero is only as good as the villains. The villain is what the hero has to overcome.

"But this movie's not about Ike. It's not about the Clantons. It's about the Earps, so the colors that I play have to be complementary to the painting that Larry wants to paint about the Earps.

"I have my feelings about what went down and how Ike was. I feel that, in the end, he didn't want the shoot-out. He was ready to leave town. And then when it did happen, of course, his brother and his buddies were killed, and he became someone else. He went on to kill. But in the shoot-out he scooted away, and in the end of the film we see something similar to that. I don't want to say he was a coward. I'm trying to give him some sense of dignity with, you know... humility. I think he realized that he and his friends were ranchers and these guys were shooters. And when it came down to it, I think Ike realized he was in over his head." —JEFF FAHEY (IKE CLANTON)

EXT. EMPTY LOT—NIGHT
CLOSE ON a whiskey bottle as it is handed around a circle of six Cowboys, including the McLaury brothers, Billy Clanton, a tough fellow named JOHNNY RINGO, and fresh-faced, young BILLY CLAIBORNE. There is a ritualistic atmosphere to the swig-taking. It is very QUIET. When the bottle has made the circuit, Frank McLaury steps away a few feet and peers off into the darkness.

FRANK'S POV. Curly Bill gives him a high sign from the corner of a building at the edge of the lot, then disappears into the shadows.

INT. ORIENTAL SALOON—NIGHT
Wyatt comes in the front, looks around casually, then sees something and heads off toward a poker table.

Doc is dealing a hand to a game of five Players. One of them, to Doc's right, is Big Nose Kate. Wyatt comes up and stands next to Doc; he stares at Kate. She doesn't look up at him. Play continues throughout.

> BIG NOSE KATE
> If you're gonna loiter like that, Wyatt, at least tell me what cards he's holding.

> WYATT
> (hard)
> I thought you left town, Kate.

> BIG NOSE KATE
> Did…went over to Globe for a while. Made love with a healthy man. Now I'm back…
> (a hand on Doc's arm in mock tenderness)
> …back with my sweet patient.

> WYATT
> That's too bad.

> DOC
> (still playing, unfazed)
> I needed her. I was enjoying life too much.

> BIG NOSE KATE
> He's just like you, Wyatt. Once he's with ya, he sticks with ya…no matter what happens.
> (finally looks up at Wyatt, like poison)
> And no matter what other people say.

> ANOTHER PLAYER
> I'm havin' trouble concentratin' here, if you don't mind.

Doc laughs, shows a hand, triumphantly.

DOC
Concentrate on these, Homer.

EXT. EMPTY LOT—NIGHT
Frank McLaury looks around at his drinking companions. He finishes the whiskey and heaves the empty bottle against a wall, where it SHATTERS loudly.

FRANK MCLAURY
Let 'er rip, boys!

The Cowboys all pull pistols and commence to FIRE AWAY into the air, WHOOPING in the manner of a legitimate "Hurrah."

EXT. SALOON DISTRICT, ALLEN STREET—NIGHT
The block, home to the majority of the town's saloons, is moderately busy. Marshal Fred White steps out from the sidewalk, looks in the direction of the distant GUNSHOTS and hurries off in that direction.

Virgil, interrupted in his rounds, comes running around the corner and heads off in the same direction.

EXT. ORIENTAL SALOON—NIGHT
Wyatt comes out the swinging doors. He locates the sounds of the disturbance and runs off in that direction.

EXT. EMPTY LOT—NIGHT
The Cowboys continue to create an uproar, but don't seem all that out of control. In fact, they keep checking the surroundings to see where the law might come from. Now three of their number begin to run off through the alley and adjoining lots, firing as they go. Frank, Tom and Billy Claiborne stay where they are, continuing to raise a ruckus.

AT THE CORNER OF THE BUILDING
Curly Bill hides, ready to take a shot at whatever lawman shows up first. Now that man appears: It is Virgil, entering the lot from the far side away from Curly Bill. Virgil, revolver in his hand, calls out to the three remaining Cowboys—

VIRGIL
That'll do it, boys! Throw up your arms!

Curly Bill is setting himself for the difficult shot at Virgil when he hears noises and turns to see Marshal White stumble into the space behind him, his Smith & Wesson revolver leveled at him. White has not seen Curly Bill's earlier posture; he takes him for one of the revelers.

MARSHAL WHITE
That'll be enough fun for now, Bill.

The Marshal has his advantage. Curly Bill raises his arms in surrender, gun still in his hand.

MARSHAL WHITE
Hand it over.

Curly Bill lowers his arm, grinning, and presents his Colt to Marshal White butt first.

CURLY BILL
Damn if you can't let off a little steam in this—

Mid-sentence, Curly Bill spins the gun in his hand, cocking it as it comes around. He FIRES into Marshal White's belly point-blank. The Marshal is blown back on his ass in the dirt.

Even Curly Bill is a little shocked by the sight. But not so shocked as a moment later, when Wyatt appears from the corner behind him and viciously WHACKS him across the skull with the barrel of his Colt. Curly Bill goes down, unconscious. Wyatt picks up Curly Bill's gun and hurries to put out the Marshal's flaming jacket as Virgil arrives on the run.

INT. JOHNNY BEHAN'S ROOMS—DAY
Johnny stands in the doorway of his bedroom, angry and disconsolate. But he's trying not to let it out. He's watching Josie move about the room, packing her suitcases.

BEHAN
You're making a big mistake, Josie.

JOSIE
I've seen the future, Johnny. You and I weren't in it.

BEHAN
I've been getting everything ready so we could be married.

Louis Smith as
Curly Bill

Jeff Fahey as
Ike Clanton

Kirk Fox as
Pete Spence

J. D. Johnston as
Frank Stillwell

Adam Baldwin as
Tom McLaury

Rex Lynn as
Frank McLaury

> JOSIE
> You been saying that since the first night you saw me in the show. But the day never came…and now it never will.
> (looks up at him)
> I'm not mad, Johnny. I think I knew about you the minute I met you. It wouldn't be right for me to marry you anyway.

> BEHAN
> Why not?

Josie strains to close her crammed suitcase, then turns and sits on the top to get it fastened.

> JOSIE
> Well, it's not just that I don't love you…
> (gets the bag snapped)
> …it's that I don't even like you.

EXT. BUNGALOW, FIRST STREET—DAY
A Teenage Boy is carrying Josie's luggage from a wagon into a little bungalow—not much more than a shack really. Josie supervises as a Real Estate Agent takes down a "For Rent " sign in the front.

INT. COURTROOM—DAY
What we HEAR throughout is the voice of Judge Wells Spicer. (The audience includes Morgan, plus a full complement of the cowboy faction.) What we SEE is faces—CLOSEUPS. First, of Curly Bill, bleary-eyed, head bandaged, mean.

> JUDGE SPICER (OS)
> …whether it all was just some drunken fun that got out of hand…whether it was an accident as you say…

Wyatt's face—seething, indignant, frustrated.

> JUDGE SPICER (OS)
> …and you were just trying to hand over your firearm when it "accidentally" discharged…

Ike Clanton's face—hard, remorseless.

> JUDGE SPICER (OS)
> …or whether this was another heinous crime against our community, carefully planned and maliciously premeditated…

Behan's face—strained, conflicted. He's been watching Ike.

> JUDGE SPICER (OS)
> …will have to wait for a jury of your peers to decide. But what we know already is this—

Virgil's face—angry, sad, staunch.

> JUDGE SPICER (OS)
> …you have robbed the people of Tombstone of a precious resource.

John Clum's face—pained. He turns to comfort Marshal White's widow—drained, spent.

> JUDGE SPICER (OS)
> … Fred White was a brave lawman, a loving father and husband…

Judge Spicer's face—outraged, disgusted, hurting.

> JUDGE SPICER
> …a loyal friend…and a good man. Which you, William Brocius, are not.
> (slams his gavel)
> Bail is set at $15,000. Virgil, you're the Acting Marshal now…take him out of my sight.

INT. ORIENTAL SALOON—DAY
Late afternoon. The place is mostly deserted. Wyatt is talking to one of the Dealers at the faro table, when he's startled by something he sees.

WYATT'S POV. Josie Marcus has come through the front doors and is hovering there hesitantly.

Wyatt comes up to her.

> WYATT
> Behan's not here.

> JOSIE
> I'm not looking for Johnny. He's horseshit.

> WYATT
> We've found something to agree on.

> JOSIE
> Maybe you've heard about the "private" photograph my former fiancé was showing around…
> (Wyatt reacts, Josie sees it)
> …or maybe you've seen it. Seems every man in town has.

Wyatt glances off, aware suddenly of the surroundings.

WYATT
You shouldn't be in here.

JOSIE
I've been in places worse than this.
(studies him a moment)
You mean you want me to go somewhere with you?

Wyatt nods. She turns and lets him hold the door for her.

EXT. MEADOW NEAR THE RIVER—SUNSET
There is a buckboard pulled up at the edge of the meadow. Josie and Wyatt walk.

JOSIE
I heard a story about you. About you and a prisoner named Tommy O'Rourke. Tommy Behind-the-Deuce they called him. Is it true what they say—how you saved him?

WYATT
People make up a lotta things. Sometimes even I don't know what really happened.
(he smiles at her)
I know this, though…the stories are always better.

JOSIE
Is Mattie Earp your wife?

WYATT
(shakes his head "no")
But we've been together a while. She uses my name. I owe her that…at the least.

JOSIE
I'm not going to marry Johnny Behan.

WYATT
I never thought you would.

JOSIE
Oh?…And what would you know about it, Mr. Earp?

WYATT
Wyatt.

JOSIE
You don't know anything about me.

WYATT
I knew a lot about you the minute you got off that stagecoach.

JOSIE
Like what?

WYATT
That you're a brave young woman. That you came out to a place like this on your own, to a man you knew wasn't right for you…because you like the adventure of it all.

Michael Madsen as Virgil Earp.

105

JOSIE
I've never been afraid of much. My family left Brooklyn, New York, in '67 and sailed around South America to get to San Francisco. I don't remember a minute of it when I was scared. When I see something new, it just gets me excited. I guess I think my whole life's gonna be like that…and I'm not afraid of it, Mr. Earp.

WYATT
You're afraid to say my name.

JOSIE
Why would I be afraid of that?

WYATT
Because you know that once you do, that'll be it.

Josie gives him a look as if he's crazy. But she's not sure she's right. She laughs.

JOSIE
You've got a lot of confidence, Mr. Ear—

She stops dead. She's caught.

WYATT
Yes?

JOSIE
I believe you're trying to seduce me.

WYATT
What do people call you?

JOSIE
Josie…

WYATT
Josie.

JOSIE
(loves him saying it, she flinches)
…What makes you different from all the
men that have tried what you're tryin'?

WYATT
I guess you know…Josie.

JOSIE
(reacts to the sound, again)
No I don't.

WYATT
Then say it.

JOSIE
All right…I don't know what you're
talking about…Wyatt.

Something happens. She flushes. He reaches
out with both arms and draws her to him. He
kisses her deeply. After a few moments, her
hands come up around his neck.

THE PERSISTENT POPULARITY OF THE WESTERN

There is something very powerful about the image of a man on a horse in a beautiful landscape. It's all about possibility. It's about self-reliance. It's about someone whose fate can turn at any moment, and about finding one's destiny in the open spaces. That's a powerful notion—that you could get on a horse and pack a saddle bag and change your life. You change your surroundings and you're not constricted by society. There's no such thing as class. It was an era in which classes were all mixed up, and the people who came to the West were people who were fleeing all the structures of society. They were trying to run away from all the European influences that dominated the Eastern side of the country. They were going to try to make a uniquely American version of society. That's a terribly attractive idea, not just to Americans but to all people—freedom. There is a liberation about being on a horse in wide-open spaces that you can make your own. You can ride out and lay claim to the land." —LAWRENCE KASDAN

I suppose it has something to do with man's instinct about being alone, being at one with nature, being on your own and being a survivor, being a strong-willed individual. I mean, that's what we see in John Wayne, isn't it? We see someone who can take care of himself and who has a great deal of integrity and doesn't start a fight but always ends one. And those are all pretty good values to lead your life by. As far as children being brought up on those values, being brought up with the idea that that's the way life should be or could be. I guess you'd have to argue whether or not that's the way we should live our life. We have a great deal of violence in the world now and maybe things shouldn't be settled with guns. But as entertainment, it gives one a great deal of scope to pursue the Western theme."
—GENE HACKMAN

I grew up in Texas, with *Gunfight at the OK Corral*, and *Shane*, and *High Noon*. There were so many of them back then, when I was growing up in the fifties and early sixties. The Western was a story of a moral code where there were rights and wrongs, and family values. And Westerns have changed and reflected our culture over the different decades. When you come into the late sixties and early seventies, you start having the anti-hero in the Western. There's no line drawn between good and evil. There's a lot of blood and guts. You have Sam Peckinpah's Westerns back then. Then they didn't make Westerns for quite a while, I think, because space became the Western. *Star Wars* was a Western. It was set in outer space, but you still had the shoot-out with the space ships. You still had that moral code that was sort of a throwback to the seventies. And now, here we are in the nineties, making Westerns again, a slew of them. I don't know if one can say what that reflects. I think maybe you need to have some time go by before you can really say what they reflect about our times." —DENNIS QUAID

I believe in the freshness of a movie. I think that a movie that is rendered correctly and told in a refreshing way will be popular in any decade, at any time. Westerns don't do very well if the Western is bad. The survival of the genre requires people to make really good, refreshing Westerns.

"But little children have always played cowboys, even when Western movies had fallen out of favor. That's because there's something terribly romantic about the idea of one man's independence, all he has are the possessions on his back, he lives by his wits. There's a code in the face of danger. We like to think that if we were faced with danger ourselves, we would face it honorably. The Western displays that idea of heroism." —KEVIN COSTNER

"Looks like Ike and Billy Clanton, the McLaurys, Billy Claiborne, maybe more." "Let's go."

EXT. STREET IN FRONT OF MINING
EXCHANGE—DAY

The Clantons, the McLaurys, and Frank Still-well are mounting up as Wyatt, Virgil, and Clum watch. The front door to the County Offices is open and as we watch, Morgan appears, roughly handling Curly Bill. When they're on the sidewalk, Morgan grabs the back of Curly Bill's pants and gives him a violent shove that sends him headfirst into the dust of the street, startling the horses and pretty much everyone else too. Curly Bill is up in an instant and turning with murder in his eyes on Morgan. Virgil steps in his path.

> VIRGIL
> Come on, Brocius. Let's go.

Curly Bill stops, looking over the Earps.

> IKE CLANTON
> Get on your horse, Bill, before they shoot you down in cold blood.
> (to Wyatt)
> You had your last chance and you let it go. There won't be any more talkin'.

Wyatt steps toward him.

> WYATT
> You talk too much for a fightin' man, Ike.

> CLUM
> (reaching for Wyatt's arm)
> Wyatt—

> WYATT
> (walks up to Ike's horse)
> I've seen your kind my whole life and there's never been but one way to deal with any of you.

> STILLWELL
> Your day is comin'. Get ready.

> DOC (OS)
> Why not make it today?

Doc crosses the street from behind the Cowboys, walking without hesitation through their mounted number and tauntingly close to Curly Bill.

> DOC
> I can't speak for everyone, but I personally am getting sick to my stomach of all your empty, yellow talk. If you want to make a fight with these boys, why not get it over with right now?

FRANK MCLAURY

You're the first on my list, Holliday. You can spend your time from now on waitin' to see me.

DOC

Seeing you would be a nice change. I understand most of your enemies got it in the back.

IKE CLANTON

We're not through.

He wheels his horse and leads his group out of town at a gallop. Virgil looks at Wyatt.

VIRGIL

What'd he mean, you had your last chance and you let it go?

Wyatt doesn't respond; he just stares after the Cowboys.

MORGAN

I think we oughta just kill 'em all.

DOC
(laughs, looks at Morgan)
You know, Morg, Wyatt's my friend, but I believe I'm beginning to love you.

INT. BEDROOM, JOSIE'S
HOUSE—DAY/NIGHT

Wyatt and Josie are under the covers. Right now, they're kissing. Not wildly, not passionately—gently, tenderly, long, exploring. They can't really get enough of the newness of it, the delight of it. It feels so good. We've caught them in the middle of a long session. The lovemaking begins and ends without clear delineation. They don't even know when they're starting again.

DISSOLVE TO:
LATER. Nothing much has changed since the previous scene. It's dark outside. A little more sweat. A little more tired. Josie lies in Wyatt's arms.

JOSIE
Now that I've found you, Wyatt, I don't want to lose you. I don't want you shot down on the street in some fight I don't even understand.

WYATT
You're not going to lose me...it's taken me too long to get here.

She kisses him.

JOSIE
I'm going to be lying here next to you when we're eighty.

WYATT
I never thought about living that long…
    (laughs softly)
but if I do, you can bet all I'll be doing is lying here.

She moves over him, kissing him hungrily.

JOSIE
We better not waste any time.

He wraps his arms around her. There is LOUD KNOCKING at the front door of the house.

EXT. JOSIE'S HOUSE—NIGHT
A few moments later. Josie has answered the door in a robe, but now stands across the room as Wyatt, barely dressed, comes up to the door to talk to Virgil.

VIRGIL
I think you better come with me, Wyatt.

INT. WYATT'S ROOMS—NIGHT
Wyatt and Virgil come into the sitting room. Allie, carrying a bowl and some cloths, is just going into the bedroom, where Mattie can be seen lying on the bed. Allie gives Wyatt a poisonous look of reproach.

ALLIE
Doc Goodfellow says she's gonna be okay. She took a dose of laudanum with her whiskey. Looks like she was trying to kill herself. Lucky we found her in time.
    (a scathing look at Wyatt)
Lucky *somebody* came around.

WYATT
Where'd she get it?

VIRGIL
Probably over in Chinatown. It's not hard to find in Tombstone.

IN THE BEDROOM. Allie settles on the bed and begins to mop Mattie's brow. Wyatt sits on the otherside. Mattie's eyes flicker open at the

movement of the bed. She sees Wyatt. Her lips move, but he can't hear what she's saying. He puts a comforting hand on her. She looks at him again, trying to speak. Wyatt leans down close to her. Her voice is a raspy whisper—

> MATTIE
> Go back to your Jew whore.

Wyatt sits up. He looks down at her, sadly, then gets up and walks out.

> ALLIE
> If I was married to him, I'd drink a gallon of that stuff.

> VIRGIL
> (harsh, for the first time)
> Allie, shut up.

INT. ORIENTAL SALOON—NIGHT
Middle of the night. So late that even here things have slowed down. Doc is playing a lazy game of poker with some other diehards when he sees Wyatt enter the saloon and walk to the end of the bar. Wyatt speaks to the Bartender, who reacts with some surprise, then fetches a bottle of whiskey and a shot glass, which he places in front of Wyatt. Wyatt takes his time opening the bottle and pouring the glass full. Doc throws in his hand and crosses to Wyatt.

Wyatt is staring at the shot glass, lost in thought. He starts to reach for it just as Doc arrives and takes the glass himself, throwing it back.

> DOC
> Don't mind if I do.

He commences to cough all over the glass, then places it back on the bar. When he stops coughing, he fills the glass again, keeping his hand on it.

> DOC
> If you're going to break the fast, the least you could do is invite a friend.

> WYATT
> Not in the mood for talking, Doc.

> DOC
> You know how it is with me…
> (throws back the second drink)
> …you don't have to do much talking when I'm around.

He pours another, very carefully, and pushes it in front of Wyatt, who just looks at it.

DOC

Wyatt, you ever wonder why we been around so many unfortunate incidents, yet we're still here walking around?
   (Wyatt is unresponsive)
I figured it out. It's nothing much…just luck. And you know why it's nothing much, Wyatt…?

Doc picks up the glass again from in front of Wyatt and drinks.

DOC

…Because it don't matter much whether we're here today or not. I wake up every morning looking in the face of Death, and you know what…? He ain't half bad.

The Bartender walks up and places a second shot glass in front of Wyatt, then leaves.

DOC

I think maybe the secret old Mr. Death is holding is that it's better for some of us over on the other side. I know it can't be

DOC (cont'd)

any worse for me. And maybe that's the place for your Mattie.

Wyatt looks up sharply at Doc. He didn't know until now that Doc knew.

DOC

For some people, this world isn't ever gonna be right.

Wyatt pours a shot into his glass and drinks it. The taste is strong and full of bad memories. He turns to Doc.

WYATT

Is that supposed to let me off the hook?

DOC

There is no hook, my friend…there's only what we do.

EXT. ALLEN STREET—NIGHT
Ike Clanton and Tom McLaury ride into town. They're grim-faced and alert to their surroundings.

COLLEEN ATWOOD, COSTUME DESIGNER

The obvious [reason that *Wyatt Earp* was an exciting opportunity] for a designer is that it's a period movie. For me it was more that it was such a great, epic story to tell. I really wanted to try to make it into something that hasn't already been made, visually I mean, the clothing, the style. I think any Western at this point, is a tribute to every great Western that's ever been made. So there are certain things that you pull from other Westerns—the best things about them— that you try to reinvent. You know, the chaps, the scarf, the hat, the boots—the real simple but functional costume of a cowboy. You try to make those things work in a new scheme.

"At that time, the cowboys, in general, dressed a lot differently than the Law. Cowboys had a gang kind of look, when they were wearing their work clothes. With the Clantons and McLaurys, I tried to keep that quality. In this story there are so many groups and sections of people that the best way to separate them was to contain each faction within a sort of style. Even though they might have had ten changes, they looked pretty much the same all the time, except for a bit of color here and there. Then you build

the background actors into the environment around them so they look like they belong there, but are still separate a little bit. The principals are usually a little stronger, there's a bit more to their look than the people walking around on the street.

"The Earps were the Law, such as it was at the time, and I look at the Earps' wardrobe, by the time we get to Dodge, as uniforms. It was the uniform of the day. When you look at the research of the lawmen, they did not want to look like cowboys. Cowboys were often their enemies, and so they separated themselves by wearing very simple clothes. Very black and white, very clean and sharp and righteous. I mean, it's not far from what a Protestant preacher wears. There's a certain righteousness about the way they dressed, and a simplicity that's very fundamental, and it sets them apart from the general citizen of the West. However, I couldn't make all of the Earps look like Wyatt. They couldn't all wear PA's [*Prince Albert jackets*] and bow ties and stand-collar shirts. I think it's been done that way but it's just too cheesy for me. When I say they wore a uniform, it doesn't mean they all looked exactly the

same. It means they all wore a white shirt and black coat. And they just looked good in different kinds of hats, so I used the shape that looked good on their heads and the size of the brims for their face. It's a character thing.

"The first thing I did when I started this movie was to start designing for Kevin. He has a really strong look, just walking into a room. I felt, with Kevin that his clothes either worked immediately or they didn't work. There was a little fine-tuning that I did with him as we went along, because you can't plan that span of time and define everything before you walk into the environment. But his general look was established first because I started with him. For Virgil, I pulled things that were more kind of straight-on, more conservative and a little different than Kevin's, and then Michael [Madsen] came in and it worked immediately. I mean, he looked so great in the clothes that his changes really fell into place easily. After that, I basically knew where I was going with Morgan.

"The women were the wild side of the period. They're definitely the color of the story. They're sort of the peacocks of the time, rather than the men. It was

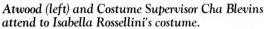
Atwood (left) and Costume Supervisor Cha Blevins attend to Isabella Rossellini's costume.

exciting to dress them because you keep layering and figuring out what colors you could put together. They were definitely a fun part of the design of the movie. Big Nose Kate was fantastic. She's the most flamboyant woman in the story. Because her past is largely undocumented, there were no restrictions of a known history. And Isabella [Rossellini]'s such a great face to put a frame around, it's hard to go wrong."

ON DOC HOLLIDAY

Doc's in a special category in my heart. I love to watch him in the movie. While his look is based on different people from the period research, it's put together in a way that I've never seen before in a movie and I like that about it. What Dennis has done to make that character work takes incredible discipline [*referring to Quaid's weight loss*], and I have nothing but really great respect for him as an actor. He wasn't, by any means, a fat person when I met him, but he looked healthy. On a good day in this movie, he looks like he's going to die. I mean, he looks really bad. And I think it's a tremendous asset to the movie. It's a great pleasure for me as a designer to be a part of what he looks like."

ON BACKGROUND AND EXTRAS

This movie has more than 120 speaking roles, a large amount for any movie, but on a period movie it's really a lot. And I'd say that, even with all those actors, the extras were at least fifty percent of mine and my crew's work. There were just so many people.

"We fit at least 1500 extras. 1500 costumes. And each one was a different character within the genre: townspeople, gamblers, ranchers, children, whatever was needed—from railroad camps to covered wagons. I mean, when you think of the towns and the number of people in each of those places, it's staggering. The demands of keeping the background operation moving are just huge. The maintenance is a major job because we have a lot of authentic clothes and a lot of reproductions in fine fabrics. There's probably six or seven hours' worth of maintenance a day just on repairs when you have a hundred extras.

"It was hard [to change the look of the extras from town to town] because, by the time we were shooting Dodge City [*near the end of the shooting schedule*], the clothes had been recycled so many times, they were falling apart on people's backs.

In some cases, we had to literally sew them on at the beginning of the day.

"The early stuff was really different because it's a different period. But when you start trying to differentiate between the historic styles of Dodge and Tombstone, it gets tricky because they were fairly close. My feeling was that Tombstone looked more finished, where the Dodge look was much rougher. It was a rougher town and there were more layers. It's a heavier kind of feeling as far as clothing goes. I also manipulated color a lot. Tombstone's much darker, more black and green, much colder colors, and Dodge has a warmer pallet, a lot of earthy colors."

KASDAN ON ATWOOD

I had never worked with Colleen before, so I was delighted that she turned out to be just extraordinarily gifted. She's done one of the most amazing jobs of anyone on this movie. She had a thorough and complete grand scheme for the long arc of the picture, but could always alter it to accommodate what I was asking for.

"She's a tough-minded, pragmatic department head and very responsible. And all within the parameters of extraordinary taste.

"She's one of the most talented costume designers I've worked with."

INT. ORIENTAL SALOON—NIGHT
Doc is playing poker and drinking heavily to quell his cough. Now he deals a hand and pours another drink from the bottle in front of him.

EXT. JOSIE'S HOUSE—NIGHT
Wyatt opens the front door from inside. Josie can be seen reading a book in a chair in the front room. They murmur their good-byes and Wyatt comes out and heads down the street.

EXT. FREMONT STREET—NIGHT
Virgil ambles among the evening crowd, making his rounds.

INT. CAMPBELL & HATCH SALOON AND BILLIARD PARLOR—NIGHT
Tom McLaury and Ike Clanton are drinking. Ike is drinking too much and starting to run off at the mouth to Bob Hatch, the bartender, and several neighboring Patrons. Tom becomes increasingly uncomfortable.

> IKE CLANTON
> …well it won't be a problem much longer. After tomorrow this town'll smell a lot better.

> TOM MCLAURY
> Come on, Ike…slow down a little, why doncha?

> IKE CLANTON
> (snapping at him)
> Don't tell me to slow down!…We've waited too long as it is. Those fucking Earps and their diseased friend are going to find out soon enough what a real fight is about.

Tom reacts with dismay to this last pronouncement. He throws some money on the bar.

> TOM MCLAURY
> I'm movin' on, Ike. If you're smart you'll go back to the hotel and get some sleep.

He walks out.

> ANOTHER PATRON
> (also well oiled)
> You're going to need some help if you're going to take on the Earps.

> IKE CLANTON
> I've got friends, you'll see that tomorrow. They're comin'. The people in this town are gonna thank us when we're done.

> BOB HATCH
> Ike, if you're gonna talk like that, you better take it somewhere else.

INT. ALHAMBRA SALOON/ OCCIDENTAL LUNCHROOM—NIGHT
The Saloon is separated from the Lunchroom by a low rail. Wyatt and Morgan enter the Lunchroom side, greet the Waitress and take a table. Morgan nods in the direction of the Alhambra bar, but Wyatt has already seen it—Ike Clanton is drinking at the bar. Wyatt focuses on the blackboard displaying the day's specials. Morgan is a little slower to take his eyes off Ike, but finally he too turns to the menu.

Doc comes steaming in the front door of the Alhambra side, looks around till he sees Ike, and makes a beeline to him. Ike is just lifting a glass to his lips when Doc swats it out of his grasp. It SHATTERS behind the bar, bringing the whole saloon to attention. Ike, startled, turns to face Doc.

> DOC
> Ike, I hear you're going to kill me. Get out your gun and commence.

> IKE CLANTON
> (showing he's unarmed)
> I ain't heeled.

> DOC
> You scum-sucking bastard, if you ain't heeled, go and arm yourself. I'll meet you in the street.
> (looks around)
> Who will give this yellow-bellied prick a gun?

Wyatt motions across their table to Morgan, who steps over the low rail and goes to the bar. Ike reacts to Morgan's arrival. He begins backing toward the door, eyes on Doc.

> IKE CLANTON
> I won't fight you tonight, Doc, but you'll get your fight soon enough.

DOC

My mama always said never put off 'til tomorrow people you can kill today.

MORGAN
(puts an arm on Doc)
Come on, Doc…he ain't armed. And he's drunk.

DOC

There ain't no law against killing drunks.

Doc yells after Ike.

DOC

If you intend to open your lying mouth about me or my friends again, then go heeled and ready to fight.

Wyatt watches it all this from his table, munching now on a biscuit.

EXT. CORNER OF ALLEN AND FOURTH—NIGHT
3 A.M. The streets are quiet.

INT. DOC'S ROOM, FLY'S BOARDING HOUSE—NIGHT
Doc stumbles drunkenly into the room, knock-

ing over a chair. Kate lifts her head from her pillow to look, then goes back to sleep.

EXT. BROTHEL—NIGHT
Tom McLaury leaves a frumpy Prostitute at the door of the seedy brothel.

INT. BEDROOM, VIRGIL'S HOUSE—NIGHT
Virgil is getting undressed as Allie watches.

VIRGIL
…so then Morgan went over and broke it up before Doc could kill Ike…or the other way around.

ALLIE
Should have let 'em go at it. Neither one amounts to much.

INT. BEDROOM, MORGAN'S HOUSE—NIGHT
Morgan comes in, his step still pretty lively considering the hour. He sits on the bed in the gloom and stares down at Lou, who sleepily stirs and opens her arms to him. Morgan is happy.

INT. SITTING ROOM, WYATT'S
ROOMS—DAY
Wyatt, shaking the sleep from his head, has
answered the door in just his pants. Josie stands
in the hallway. Wyatt steps outside and closes
the door.

INT. HALLWAY, WYATT'S BOARDING
HOUSE—DAY
Josie comes into Wyatt's arms in the dim hall-
way.

> WYATT
> Josie, what are you doing here?

> JOSIE
> Ike Clanton's been going around all
> morning saying they're going to shoot
> the first Earp who shows his face.

> WYATT
> Just Ike?

> JOSIE
> ("no")
> Wyatt, come away with me now. We'll
> leave all the troubles behind and go.

> WYATT
> What are you talking about?

> JOSIE
> I'll go anywhere you want. We could
> leave tonight…you and me.

> WYATT
> Leave? I'm not gonna leave.

> JOSIE
> Wyatt, please. I don't want to see you
> shot down in some street fight I don't
> even understand.

Wyatt just looks at her.

> WYATT
> Have you seen my brothers?
>   (Josie shakes her head "no")
> I have to go.

Josie speaks to his back, full voice.

> JOSIE
> Wyatt, you don't owe this town a thing.

Wyatt stops.

INT. BEDROOM, WYATT'S
ROOMS—NIGHT
Wyatt has just come in. He stands in the doorway looking over at the sprawled form of Mattie
on the bed—drugged, drunk, snoring.

EXT. FREMONT STREET—NIGHT
At first, just shadows and light. Then, from the
darkness, Ike Clanton. His eyes burn. He can't
sleep. He's sobering up. WE PUSH IN on him
and begin—

A SLOW DISSOLVE INTO THE LIGHT OF:
EXT. THIRD STREET—DAY
Frank McLaury, Billy Clanton, and Billy Clai-
borne ride up Third and turn onto Allen Street.

WYATT

This is where we live, my brothers and me. We've staked it all on this place.

JOSIE

It's nothing, Wyatt. It's a mining camp. Dirty and small-minded.

WYATT

It's our home and I'm not leaving, Josie. Not for the Clantons or the McLaurys or anybody, not even you.

This stops Josie cold. After a long pause—

JOSIE

Then give me a gun…and let me stand with you. I'll kill anyone that tries to hurt you. Give me a gun.

Wyatt smiles slowly.

WYATT

Go home, Josie. Thinking about you could get me killed.

He turns to go.

JOSIE

Wyatt…I love you, Wyatt.

She watches him carefully here to see the effect of her words.

JOSIE

I love you more than I'll ever love anyone as long as I live.

Wyatt says nothing. It's impossible to know what he is thinking, but Josie has finally said what everybody in the world needs to hear.

JOSIE

I'll go home now.

INT. SITTING ROOM/BEDROOM, WYATT'S ROOMS—DAY

Wyatt comes back in from the hall and closes the door. He looks up to find Mattie standing in the bedroom doorway. She's a wreck, half-drugged, out of control. But she starts with a quiet intensity that's scary.

MATTIE

If you leave me, I'll kill myself. I'll do it this time. I swear, swear before God almighty I'll kill myself, and it'll be on your head!

Wyatt gives her a look, then brushes by her as he goes into the bedroom.

MATTIE

Do you hear me? If you don't break off with that whore, you'll come back and find me dead.

Wyatt begins dressing.

MATTIE

Talk to me, you cold-hearted son of a bitch!

Wyatt stops and meets her gaze. His voice is calm.

WYATT

There are men out there I may have to kill, Mattie…I don't have time for this today.

EXT. FRONT PORCH, VIRGIL'S HOUSE —DAY

Virgil comes out into the chill of the day. He looks around, careful as he exits the house. He's down the walk before Allie comes out and stands

on the porch. He gives her a little, reassuring smile as he closes the front gate. She just looks at him. She's pretty tough, but she's scared.

INT. DOC'S ROOM, FLY'S BOARDING HOUSE—DAY
Big Nose Kate shakes Doc awake. It isn't easy.

BIG NOSE KATE
Doc, wake up! Ike Clanton was around looking for you and he was armed.

Doc rolls over. Even on a good morning this is not a pleasant sight; today, hungover, he looks like Mr. Death himself. He comes slowly to life, digesting Kate's words. Sits up with agonizing effort.

DOC
If God will let me live long enough, Ike will see me.

EXT. FREMONT STREET—DAY
Wyatt, still shaking off his grogginess in the cool air, approaches the corner of Third. A Townsman stops him and speaks, vaguely indicating the direction of the business district ahead. Wyatt already knows, but he thanks him and moves on. Morgan is coming down Third from his

house. Wyatt sees him and they fall into step.

MORGAN
You heard?

WYATT
(nods)
You know how many?

MORGAN
("no")
I wonder if Curly Bill and those boys come in.

Wyatt doesn't know, doesn't seem to care. He'll take what comes. They turn the corner onto Fourth Street.

EXT. ORIENTAL SALOON, CORNER OF ALLEN AND FOURTH—DAY
As Wyatt and Morgan walk diagonally down the block toward the saloon, Virgil comes out of the Wells Fargo Depot checking the load in a double-barreled shotgun. The three brothers meet and walk up onto the sidewalk in front of the Oriental. From here they command a view in four directions. The Passersby are very aware of something about to happen. They cluster in little groups up the block.

WYATT
What do you hear?

VIRGIL
Ike's been up all night drinkin', tryin' to screw up the courage to kill us. Billy Clanton, Frank McLaury, and Billy Claiborne came in this morning.

MORGAN
Curly Bill…Stillwell?

VIRGIL
Don't know. Could be anybody's here.

WYATT
Where's Holliday?

VIRGIL
Hasn't been around.

WYATT
(nods)
Let him sleep.

VIRGIL
How do you want to handle this, Wyatt?

WYATT
(turning to the saloon)
I'm going to have some coffee.

INT. ORIENTAL SALOON—DAY
This is the beginning of the scene that we saw at the start of movie. The light from the entrance dominates the gloom of the saloon, silhouetting Wyatt. CLEM HAFFORD, the bartender, pours him a cup of coffee at the bar.

WYATT
Why don't you give me one of those cigars.

Hafford gives him one. Wyatt bites off the end and lights up.

HAFFORD
Is there gonna be a fight, Wyatt?

WYATT
(slowly, after a moment)
I think there must be.

Wyatt takes his coffee and goes over to the table at which we first saw him, his back to us.

(In fact, this is the same shot that started the film.) Wyatt takes off his hat, then removes the Colt from his holster and checks it.

HAFFORD
Do you want some help?

WYATT
("no")
Thanks, Clem.

Hafford accepts that and goes back to his work behind the bar. Wyatt lays the Colt on the table.

Morgan and Virgil come in and walk up to Wyatt.

MORGAN
They just moved out of the O.K. Corral… down by Fly's.

Wyatt nods.

VIRGIL
Looks like Ike, Billy, the McLaurys, and Billy Claiborne. Maybe more.

Wyatt takes the Colt from the table, puts on his hat, and gets up.

WYATT

Let's go.

The three men go out the swinging door into the blinding sunlight. But this time, WE GO WITH THEM.

EXT. FOURTH STREET—DAY
The Earps start up Fourth toward Fremont.

DOC (OS)

Where the hell you going?

Doc comes across from the opposite corner. He's wearing a long coat against the cold and uses a walking stick; he looks more infirm than ever, but his voice is strong.

WYATT

We're going down the street.

DOC

I think I'll join you.

VIRGIL

We intend to disarm them and take them in. Do you understand that, Doc?

Doc gives Virgil a look, taking in the shotgun Virgil carries.

DOC

Sure, I understand, Virgil. But do you think they will?

Virgil hands Doc the shotgun and takes Doc's walking stick in return.

VIRGIL

Put that under your coat and keep it there. No use provokin' 'em before we get a chance to talk.

Doc cradles the shotgun in his left arm under his coat. With his right hand he checks his nickel-plated Colt in its holster. The four men head up Fourth again.

MORGAN

Hell, I've heard too much talk already.

EXT. FREMONT STREET—DAY
The four reach the corner and turn left onto Fremont. Wyatt and Virgil walk in front of Morgan and Doc. The whole town seems to know what's happening now. Little knots of Townspeople move jerkily along the sidewalks

and alleys, simultaneously attracted by the excitement and fearful of getting too close. There will be a great many witnesses to what transpires down the block.

Down the block, at the front of the small vacant lot between Fly's Boarding House and the Harwood residence, Johnny Behan has been talking to the Cowboys. As the Earps and Holliday walk down the block in that direction, Behan breaks away from the Cowboys and hurries toward the Earp group, which does not slow down.

BEHAN

Don't go down there or there'll be trouble.

VIRGIL

I am going to disarm them.

BEHAN

There's no need for that. I've disarmed them.

WYATT

Then there won't be any trouble, Johnny.

Behan falls behind the group, ineffectual. He follows at a distance, shading toward the entrance to Fly's. As they pass Bauer's Butcher Shop, almost to the lot, Morgan speaks quietly to Doc on his right.

MORGAN

Let 'em have it.

DOC

All right.

The street is emptying fast as Townspeople get the word and scurry for cover. (We become aware of several of their vantage points and the Fight, when seen from a distance, will be from their POVs: a second-floor window; down the block fifty yards; from the window of Fly's Boarding House.)

EXT. THE VACANT LOT—DAY
As the Earps and Holliday reach the vacant lot, Morgan and Doc come around Wyatt and Virgil to form a line roughly across the street end of the lot. Arrayed across from them in another straggly line are Ike Clanton, Billy Claiborne (deeper in the lot), Tom McLaury standing with his horse, then Billy Clanton and, finally, Frank

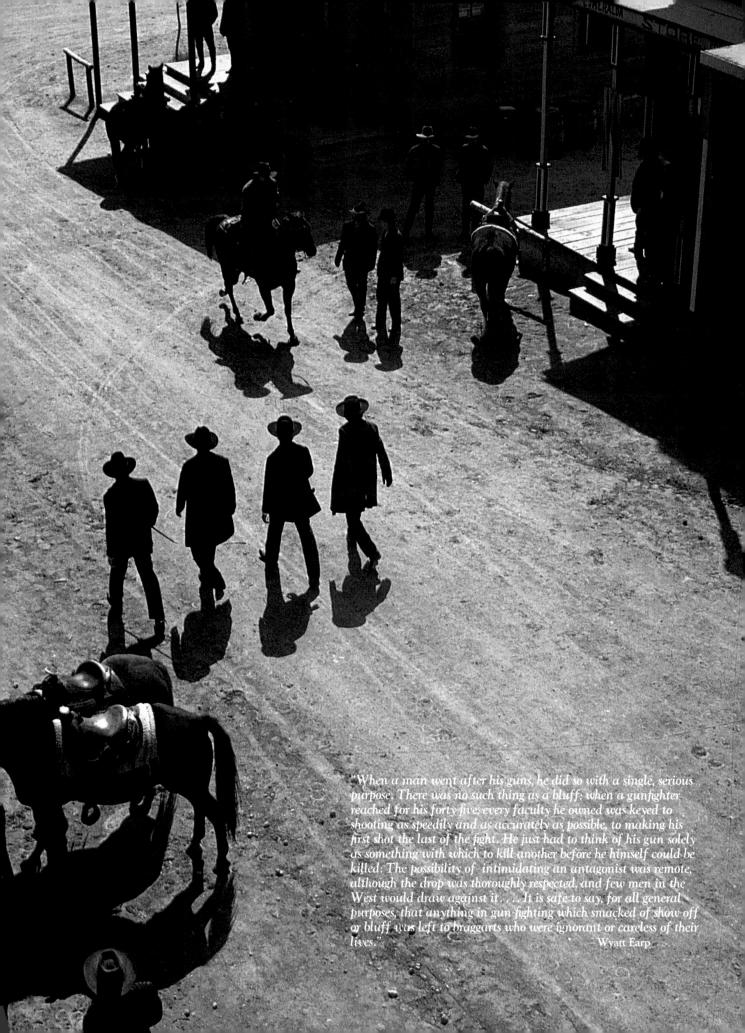

"When a man went after his guns, he did so with a single, serious purpose. There was no such thing as a bluff; when a gunfighter reached for his forty-five, every faculty he owned was keyed to shooting as speedily and as accurately as possible, to making his first shot the last of the fight. He just had to think of his gun solely as something with which to kill another before he himself could be killed. The possibility of intimidating an antagonist was remote, although the drop was thoroughly respected, and few men in the West would draw against it. . . . It is safe to say, for all general purposes, that anything in gun-fighting which smacked of show-off or bluff was left to braggarts who were ignorant or careless of their lives."
—Wyatt Earp

McLaury, holding his horse. The two groups are only a few feet apart.

There is no pause. The Earps have barely arrived when—

> MORGAN
> You sons of bitches have been looking for a fight, now you can have it.

Virgil throws a sharp glance at Morgan, then speaks to the Cowboys.

> VIRGIL
> Throw up your hands. I want your guns.

The next thirty seconds are a shocking, violent, scary mess. In this tiny little space, with the combatants only feet apart, THIRTY SHOTS ARE FIRED. It's almost impossible with the naked eye to tell the order of things—who did what and when. The SOUND IS DEAFENING, the horses WHINNY and rear, and gunsmoke rapidly fills the air, making it even harder to follow the action, which has begun with Virgil's demand. What we see, or almost see, or see from the confusing distance of some of the witnesses, is this—

Morgan and Doc suddenly have their revolvers up and pointing.

Billy Clanton and the McLaurys are reaching for their guns.

Wyatt draws with incredible speed and eerie calm. Virgil shouts once more—

> VIRGIL
> Hold, I don't mean that!

Billy Claiborne runs off toward Fly's Photo Gallery, behind the Boarding House. Morgan, Doc, and Wyatt all open fire, as do

Billy Clanton and Frank McLaury. Frank and Billy immediately take hits. Frank's horse, panicked by the shooting, starts to pull him into the street. Bleeding from a stomach wound, Frank is still able to maintain his balance and use the moving horse as a shield as he moves into the street. He fires under the horse's neck at the opposition.

Billy Clanton takes a shot in the chest which throws him against the wall of the Harwood house. Almost immediately, he is hit again in the wrist. But rather than losing his gun, he shifts it to his left hand and again begins to FIRE AWAY. Hit twice already, he continues to fight with amazing grit.

Incredibly, Ike, who is right next to Wyatt, throws open his coat, revealing he is unarmed.

IKE CLANTON
Don't shoot me, Wyatt! I'm unarmed, I swear! Don't shoot!

Wyatt, whose gun is momentarily pointed at Ike, doesn't know whether to believe him. In that instant, Ike grabs Wyatt's gun arm, forcing it down. Wyatt throws Ike off; Ike rushes into the front of the Boarding House. The wood above Wyatt's head EXPLODES from a shot from Billy Clanton. Wyatt fires at Billy, who is blocked from view by Tom's horse.

Morgan has turned his back on the lot to fire at Frank out in the street. Tom McLaury shoots Morgan in the shoulder, knocking him down. A shot from Wyatt grazes the horse at Tom's side and the horse bolts out into the street.

Doc holsters his revolver and brings out the shotgun as Tom McLaury levels his gun at Doc's face. Doc fires one barrel into Tom's side. The force blows him off his feet, but incredibly he staggers back up and starts out into the street in a death wander. Doc fires the other barrel of the shotgun after him, missing, then throws the shotgun down and draws his pistol again. Tom collapses in the dust of the street.

WYATT EARP

158 EXT, THE VACANT LOT DAY

SC 158

MORGAN, DOC AND WYATT ALL OPEN FIRE -

"THEY JUST MOVED OUT OF THE OK CORRAL..."

In junior high, we'd all heard that there was going to be a fight after school. Two guys who were pretty tough somehow decided that at the end of the day they were going to fight. There's a lot of tension in the air. The tension was very high all day, all six periods. Then you go off campus somewhere and it gets going and suddenly it's real. You thought to yourself, 'Oh, it's just talk', and the next thing you knew, there were fists flying and blood and somebody was really hurt. And you thought, 'Man, it was coming all day and then it came.'

"Most fights don't live up to the expectations, but I think this one did. The OK Corral had been coming for a while, and more specifically, the sequence of events show that it had been coming all day. I believe that those guys went down there and hung out at Fly's by the OK Corral because they were waiting for Doc, probably to assassinate him. That's where Doc lived. So you can imagine their surprise when they saw four of them walking down there. They thought they were going to face one guy and the next thing they knew they were facing four, and two of them were Doc Holliday and Wyatt Earp. They must have felt their mistake at that moment, along with a sudden shift of confidence.

"I believe Wyatt and Doc saw what was coming and decided that instead of getting picked off in the next two or three nights, they we're going to go down there and get it over with. And nobody like Johnny Behan could do anything about it. It was too late. So what's fantastic is to know that the tension existed all day and that they walked the whole streets of the town to get there." —KEVIN COSTNER

In terms of elemental effects, that was a big sequence for dust and smoke, because you have to continue to build those as the gunfight continues because in those days they all used 3f powder in their bullets instead of the smokeless powder we use. But in terms of gunshot-wound effects, [all of our work] depends on how graphic the director wants the blood-hits to be, which ones he thinks should be graphic and which he thinks should be subtle. The Frank McClaury forehead hit was probably be the most graphic. It was also difficult to film because we had to coor-

dinate with a relatively complicated stunt— hobbling, then falling over backward. But by the end of the actual shoot-out, three people die and three people are wounded— the three good guys being the ones that are wounded. Then it's just a matter of trying to mix and match between the director of makeup effects for the prosthetics, wardrobe for the clothes, and the director of photography for what we could get away with, how big we could get. We always try to push for bigger, better, but a lot of times we had to tone down to what everybody else needs and for what the picture requires."

—BURT DALTON,
SPECIAL EFFECTS COORDINATOR

The Gunfight at the OK Corral is the most remembered, talked-about gunfight in the history of the West. There has to be a reason for that, there has to be a reason why it was remembered. I think it's because it was a family, because it was three brothers together, and their friend, Doc Holliday. You put three brothers together with a friend and they all walked down the street together. They go after some guys. Let's face it, that's pretty compelling. It's people looking out for each other, which is getting more rare every day."

—MICHAEL MADSEN (VIRGIL)

The conflict between the Earps and McLaurys started not specifically with those two groups. There was a company called the Clark and Grey Company and it was a town-site company that had been put together, as required by law, in order to buy deeds from the U.S. Government. And according to the historians, there were two factions in Tombstone. There was the cowboy faction, that were hired to do a lot of the messy work for the Clark and Grey Company. Then there was the other side—the townspeople—and the Earps, as the law, fell on the side of the townspeople. The cowboys, on behalf of their employers Clark and Grey, were occasionally hired to do some fairly ugly work. Sometimes they would burn buildings. Sometimes they would force tenants to pay rent that they really shouldn't have paid. So there was a lot of animosity toward the cowboys on the part of the townspeople, which maybe should really have been directed at the Clark

and Grey Company. But the Earps happened to be on the townspeople's side, and so I think all that caused a lot of conflict with everybody, not just the Earps and the Clanton/McLaurys gang. There was a large population of cowboy supporters and a large population of townspeople supporters, and I think there wasn't specifically any incident that led to the conflict. It was the whole political atmosphere of that town at that time. Tensions were very high, so a clash like this was waiting to happen.

"To tell the truth, I think the Earps had as much dark as the Clantons and the McLaurys really. I think it was just four of them happened to be hired to steal cattle and rob trains and four of them happened to be hired to wear a badge."

—REX LYNN (FRANK MCLAURY)

When you talk about the authenticity of a picture, it's asinine to believe that a hundred and forty years ago there were guys who were seventy or eighty yards apart, and with a single shot they were down. It just didn't happen that way. The guns weren't as refined as they are today. The truth is that these guys came face to face. In the OK Corral, they're only yards apart. They came to meet and to talk, and then it exploded from there. These guys were only three or four yards apart." —JIM WILSON, PRODUCER

A large part of the appeal of this particular Western, of Wyatt Earp's story, is that it's very much a family story. There were hundreds of gunfights, many of them famous, but none more famous than the Gunfight at the OK Corral. I think that one of the reasons is that there were three brothers walking down the street with their friend. And the friendship [with Doc Holliday] is terribly important; it was sort of an adjunct to the family, like an adopted black sheep.

"These three brothers and their friend went down to face the enemy and I think that's why the gunfight looms so large in our mythology, because that's what everyone dreams of—a family that will be with you to the death. A family that will stand beside you in the worst circumstance."

—LAWRENCE KASDAN

Billy Clanton, slumped now against the wall of Harwood's, fires across the lot at Virgil, hitting him in the calf. Virgil falls to one knee and proceeds to return fire.

Wyatt aims at Billy across the lot—takes that deliberate fraction of a second longer than we expect—and fires. Billy is hit. His revolver goes still in his lap.

Frank's horse rears and finally bucks itself free and runs off toward Fourth Street, leaving the wounded Frank exposed for the first time. For an instant he has Doc's advantage. He shoots Holliday in the hip, the bullet grazing off Doc's holster and skimming his back. Doc goes to his knees; his return shot at Frank goes wide.

Wyatt, deepest in the lot and farthest from Frank, takes aim at Frank just as Morgan raises up on an elbow to fire at him too. The brothers' guns go off simultaneously. Frank is hit in the head and is dead before he hits the ground.

IT'S OVER. Suddenly, it is QUIET. It has taken less time to happen than it takes to read about here. Billy Clanton, Tom and Frank McLaury are dead. Morgan, Doc and Virgil have been hit.

Wyatt is unscathed.

EXT. FREMONT STREET—DAY
MINUTES LATER. A large crowd of Townspeople, including China Mary and a knot of Chinese, have gathered to watch, gossip and help clean up the battlefield. Morgan, wounded and hurting but conscious, is taken away in the back of a buckboard with both Lou and a Doctor attending him. Virgil, hit in the calf, is helped up into a wagon by Allie and Wyatt, whose shirt front is covered with blood. When that wagon rolls off, Wyatt stands looking after it a moment.

Johnny Behan and one of his Deputies come up to Wyatt.

> BEHAN
> Wyatt, I'm takin' you in.

> WYATT
> (to the wagon driver)
> Don't move him too much. Take him down to the house.

> BEHAN
> Wyatt, I'm going to have to arrest you.

Wyatt turns to look at Behan. It's frightening. Behan shrinks back a step.

> WYATT
> Johnny, I won't be arrested by you or anybody else today.

Behan has drawn his gun. Wyatt has his hand on his Colt. At that moment, John Clum steps between them.

> CLUM
> In the name of God, Wyatt, there's been enough blood for one day!

Wyatt turns away, in the direction his brothers have gone. He has taken only a few steps when Josie emerges from the hubbub and flies into his arms. Behan seems to wince at the display. Josie reacts with alarm to the blood on his shirt.

> JOSIE
> Wyatt, are you all right…?

> WYATT
> I'm okay, Josie. You go home now…you hear?

> JOSIE
> No…I want to be with you now.

> WYATT
> Josie, go *home*…. It might not be over.
> (turns to Clum)
> John, will you see her home?

> CLUM
> Miss Marcus, Wyatt's right. Please…

Clum leads Josie away. Behind them a fight is brewing between Clem Hafford and a Clanton supporter, a Rancher. The crowd seems split in its assessment.

> RANCHER
> They murdered 'em. Them Earps killed 'em in cold blood!

> HAFFORD
> Ike Clanton's been in here threatening to kill 'em all morning. It was a fair fight.

As they start to get physical, Behan moves to intercede. Wyatt backs away.

INT. LIVING ROOM, VIRGIL'S HOUSE—DAY

Chaos. The room is jammed with Earps (James and Bessie have now joined the group) and their milling Allies. Morgan has been laid out on a bed that's been brought into the living room. Virgil is in his own bed in the other room. Doctor Goodfellow has been working on Morgan, but now leaves him to take a look at Virgil. Lou hovers on the bloody bed next to Morgan, near hysteria. Other people come in carrying mattresses. They're setting the house up to be defended against attack, but the tiny place is already getting claustrophobic.

Wyatt comes into the house. In his arms is Mattie, near comatose.

> WYATT
> Everybody who's not family, get out.

The supporters start to file out. Allie comes out of the bedroom.

> WYATT
> Allie, push that chair over here for her.

> ALLIE
> Don't tell me what to do in my house.

> WYATT
> (trying to control himself)
> Allie…it doesn't matter what you think of me. But men may be coming into town to kill us all before this day is through. We have to cooperate with each other—
> (losing it)
> —so get me the damned chair!

Allie jumps at this. The room goes silent. Allie clears off the chair and pushes it over. Wyatt puts Mattie gently into it.

> BESSIE
> What happened to her?

> WYATT
> (holds up bottle)
> This…a lot of it.

Lou has been staring at Wyatt. Now she rises from the bed in a rage.

LOU

It's your fault this happened. I wanted to get away from here, but he wouldn't leave you. You and the precious brothers. Well damn you to hell, Wyatt Earp!

She surprises everyone, even herself, by suddenly slapping Wyatt hard.

EXT. VIRGIL'S HOUSE—NIGHT
All the windows have been covered from inside. No light escapes.

INT. LIVING ROOM, VIRGIL'S HOUSE —NIGHT
Hell on earth—hot, stuffy, unbearably close. Morgan sleeps fitfully, his dressing stained with blood. A fly BUZZES through the room, then lands on the bloody bandages. Lou, half-awake beside Morgan, waves the fly away. Mattie sits staring forlornly into space.

Weapons are stacked against the wall. Wyatt peers out through the cracks between the mattresses. James is lying with Bessie on a mattress on the floor. He's fallen asleep holding a whiskey bottle. Now Bessie pries it from his grasp and takes a swig, looking around in disgust.

BESSIE

Well, here we are…one big happy family.

At the window, Wyatt's eyes look like deep, dark pits.

EXT. TOMBSTONE—SUNRISE
The town, seen from the surrounding desert, as the sun peeks over the hills.

DISSOLVE TO:
The word: MURDER, the letters filling the screen from edge to edge, as we PAN and PULL BACK to reveal:

EXT. FRONT WINDOW, RITTER & REAM, CITY UNDERTAKERS—DAY
The word is part of a long horizontal sign that crosses three upright, open coffins. The sign reads—"MURDERED ON THE STREETS OF TOMBSTONE." In the coffins are the McLaurys and Billy Clanton.

INT. DOC'S ROOM, FLY'S BOARDING HOUSE—DAY
Big Nose Kate lovingly applies a dressing to an ugly surface wound that runs across Doc's lower back. He is lying on his stomach diagonally across the bed so he can keep his hands on a bottle of whiskey on the floor.

EXT. ALLEN STREET—DAY
Moving Black Shapes in slow dirge-like motion. Now it becomes clear what they are: the Participants in a large Funeral Procession bearing the bodies of the McLaurys and Billy Clanton to their final rest. Many of the Participants are clearly Cowboys come into town to pay their respects, but there are many Townspeople as well. A few carry signs denouncing the "Murder" and calling for "Justice in Tombstone."

Wyatt stands among a group of his Allies on a raised sidewalk watching as the procession passes. *Ike Clanton, Frank Stillwell, Pete Spence and Curly Bill Brocius cast deadly stares at Wyatt as they pass.*

EXT. VIRGIL'S HOUSE—DAY
Johnny Behan stands across the street from the house nervously watching this scene—

John Clum and one of Behan's men, DEPUTY BLACK, stand waiting outside the house, surrounded by Earp Allies. Wyatt and Doc come out. They see Behan across the way and give him a contemptuous look. Wyatt nods to Clum.

CLUM
Wyatt…Doc.

WYATT
John…What are you doing here with him?

CLUM
Wyatt, I'm here as your friend. We have warrants for you and Doc, Morgan and Virgil, for the crime of murder. Your brothers can stay here while they recover, but—
(indicating Black)
—he's here to take you in.
(glances over at Behan)
Behan was afraid if he came down here with his deputies, there'd be bloodshed.

DOC
Johnny's not as dumb as I thought.

CLUM
I told him he was a fool. That you believe in law and justice and that any trial will vindicate you.

WYATT
Law and justice aren't necessarily the same thing in this part of the country.

CLUM
You have friends, Wyatt. We'll make your bail and get you the best attorney. But the warrants are legal.

WYATT
I won't let them use the law to kill me and my family, John. I won't allow that.

EXT. FRONT ENTRANCE, COSMOPOLITAN HOTEL—MAGIC HOUR
The Earps are moving everyone into this small hotel for security. Morgan is carried into the hotel on a stretcher; the younger Earp is in high spirits, recovering nicely, joking with the men who carry him. Lou, Allie, James and Bessie are bringing in luggage. Virgil, limping, moves

among several Earp Allies who carry rifles and keep an eye out.

Wyatt comes up the street supporting a woozy Mattie.

MATTIE
I don't want to go to no hotel, Wyatt…

WYATT
We're all going, Mattie.

MATTIE
Where's my medicine? Did you take my medicine?

INT. LOBBY, COSMOPOLITAN HOTEL—MAGIC HOUR
Wyatt leads Mattie into the crowded lobby. Mattie looks up and sees Josie coming down the stairway. Mattie tries to break from Wyatt's grasp to attack Josie.

MATTIE
Noooooo! You sonuvabitch, you brought your whore!

JOSIE
(standing her ground)
I won't stay under the same roof with that…

WYATT
Enough!

Everyone freezes. Doc and Big Nose Kate are at the front entrance, bags in tow, and have witnessed everything. Kate looks at Doc.

"I WON'T STAY UNDER THE SAME ROOF WITH THAT…"

I think it takes two people [for a relationship to fail]. It's not that Wyatt dismissed Mattie, but that at a certain point, when you're around anyone who needs you that much, it begins to drain you. It's like an albatross around your neck. The trouble is, when your own relationship [begins to crumble], you are almost helpless. You don't know how to rekindle it. You don't know how to break it off. You don't know what to do. You don't even know what the right thing to do is. I think she was a very, very needy person. I think Wyatt was a one-woman person. I think he was with Mattie and decided to stay with her, not to dally around. That was not his way. And their relationship was convenient. I think that because Wyatt was a guy of pretty recognizable character, people came to think of Mattie as his woman, and it was hard to dissociate that. It was probably not like him to abandon her when he might have wanted to. I think that there was a downward spiral, a helplessness that Mattie must have felt.

"Then a woman came into his life who affected him in a very strong way. She discombobulated him a little bit and said things to him that he found disconcerting. There was an oddness that he had not known with any other woman. And when you combine those things with being attractive, it's a very sexy thing. And it was something that he ultimately could not resist."

—KEVIN COSTNER

Once I started to logically pick apart [Wyatt and Mattie's relationship], I remember the first question I asked Larry at rehearsal was, 'Is Mattie aware of Wyatt's problems in his heart with working women?' I remember Larry saying, 'No.' [And I remember] thinking, 'Well, wait a minute then. If she's not aware, okay, that's good to know. Then her obsession with him and his rejection would be doubly puzzling if she had no idea that he rejected all prostitutes.' Because that meant I could really even go further. What Larry wrote, if you look at it, is an incredibly confident person, in that when she starts to figure out that she's not getting him and that he won't ever be hers, instead of crumbling, she gets angry. She gets really, really, angry. When a person says, 'I'm going to kill myself but it's going to be on your head,' you can't question that she's got a spirit. I thought, 'He's written a woman who's being destroyed and her sense of herself is being destroyed because she's totally defining herself through him.' She's saying, 'I can be whatever you want,' and yet she's a woman who started with some strength. That was really pleasing to me."

—MARE WINNINGHAM

I think Josie was really a perfect match for Wyatt, in terms of energy and adventurousness. She had this independent streak. They lived together for forty years and they did a lot of different things together. They had different businesses—saloons, they owned racehorses, they traveled to Alaska during the Gold Rush. I think she really matched him in a kind of wanderlust.

"She was the type of woman who spotted the 'top guy' and was attracted to that power. That was what Johnny Behan was when she first met him, and that was what Wyatt was when they got involved. Powerful men became goals for her. The way I've experienced her, she was not manipulating, but she certainly set her goals and went for them. I think she had the same kind of determination that Wyatt did, and I think they recognized that in each other. She was as stubborn as he was.

"Also—something that was very unique about Josie for a woman of her time—she had a very defined sense of herself and did not define herself by the man that she was with. She knew who she was already, because she made these huge choices early in her life. She says to Wyatt, 'Come play with me. If you don't love me, I'm not going to fall apart the way Mattie does, but I sure would like to play with you.'"

—JOANNA GOING

He didn't have the strength to break off his relationship with Mattie. The same qualities of loyalty, fierce loyalty, that rule his life make it impossible for him to break off with her. So he winds up, instead, torturing her by never being able to give her what she wants, which is his love. She imposes herself into his life. He's not a good husband or lover for her and it ended tragically for her, a suicide. Wyatt is a guy who wants to do the right thing, all the time. That's the 'responsibility' side of him. But it brings conflict with his desires. Mattie is at the heart of that. What he really should do is let her go, and yet he can't. He feels responsible to her.

"What he gave up with the death of Urilla was the hope of true romantic excitement. I think he thought he would never be excited that way again. When Josie comes into his life, she's only 19 years old. She represents a rebirth for him, a second chance, the belief that love could happen. That he wouldn't live in a compromised state the way he saw [his brother] James, that he wouldn't be part of the netherworld of whores and gamblers. She was some fresh wind blowing into a life that seemed as if it had seen its last. And then she professed and acted on her absolute devotion to him, and that sort of unconditional love is almost irresistible. She is what's drawing him away from his responsibility with Mattie. It's his absolute desire, his sensual desire for her, which is stronger than any kind of rational thinking. And she makes it very easy and appealing and says, 'I don't care if people know about us because I want you.' And she was an enormously attractive person. She was beautiful and sensual and young. And it turned out to be real. They were together for 40 years. She was game. She was game for whatever he wanted, which turned out to be a very turbulent life of almost constant travel, almost no roots and, despite their efforts, no children."

—LAWRENCE KASDAN

BIG NOSE KATE

Oh no...You're not cooping me up with all of them. I'll take my chances with the Clantons.

Kate turns on her heels and walks away. Doc watches her go. Josie heads back through the lobby and Wyatt half-carries Mattie upstairs.

EXT. FREMONT STREET—DAY

Townspeople look on in wonder at a sight they never expected to see: There, being marched down the street in a little procession that includes Behan, Deputy Black, Clum, and Doc Holliday, is Wyatt Earp, being taken off to jail.

INT. JAIL CELL, CITY JAIL—NIGHT

Wyatt and Doc are in a cell together. Wyatt lies on his bunk staring at the ceiling. Doc has his deck of cards.

DOC

Wyatt, you're taking this too seriously.
    (no response)
I know it's your first time on this side of the bars, but—

WYATT

It's not.

DOC

Come again?

WYATT

It's not my first time. I was in jail in Arkansas...a long time ago.

DOC

What'd you do...break the Sabbath?

WYATT

Horse theft.

DOC

Horse theft! Wyatt, I'm shocked. Did you do time?

WYATT

No. I ran.

DOC

I *am* shocked.
    (looks over at him)
And impressed.

INT. WELLS SPICER'S COURTROOM—DAY

An extended SERIES OF SHOTS, encompassing the many days of testimony in the Inquest. The courtroom is filled to capacity. As the CAMERA GLIDES slowly around the room, the Witnesses change, the Crowd changes, the Principal Players appear in different outfits, each moment DISSOLVING into another. Taking their turns on the witness stand, energetically making their points or quietly offering testimony, we see—Ike Clanton, Billy Claiborne, Johnny Behan, Wyatt, Virgil, Clem Hafford, and Various Witnesses we saw on the day of the Gunfight.

The last shot of this series begins at the back of the crowded courtroom and MOVES STEADILY IN on Wells Spicer on the bench as he reads his decision. Everyone is focused on him, every word matters. As we get closer, the MUSIC we've been hearing FADES AWAY and we hear—

JUDGE SPICER

...in view of the controversies between the Earps and the Clantons and the McLaurys, and the quarrel the night before between Isaac Clanton and John Holliday, I am of the opinion that the defendant, Virgil Earp, as chief of police, subsequently calling on his brothers and John Holliday to assist him in arresting and disarming the Clantons and the McLaurys—committed an injudicious and censurable act...
    (some reaction from the crowd)
...yet when you consider the existence of a law-defying element in our midst
...and consider the many threats that have been made against the Earps, I can attach no criminality to his unwise act.
    (more reaction)
...Moreover, the evidence taken before me, in this case, would not, in my judgment, warrant a conviction of the defendants by trial jury...of any offense whatever.
    (rising reaction)

I order the defendants to be released.

There is general relief around the Defendants' table. Wyatt and Doc exchange a serious look;

neither goes for showing much in public. Wyatt stands and turns to look into the crowd.

WYATT'S POV. Josie rises from her seat in the audience. She's very relieved. Several rows behind her, Wyatt takes in the angry, hostile exit of Ike Clanton, Frank Stillwell, Curly Bill, Johnny Ringo, and some of their Allies. They look his way, their glares holding the promise of future trouble.

Wyatt shows nothing.

EXT. CAMPBELL & HATCH SALOON AND BILLIARD PARLOR—NIGHT
Stormy night, rain and wind. Wyatt, Morgan, and their friend SHERM McMASTERS come down the sidewalk from the direction of the Oriental Saloon. McMasters goes into the billiard parlor. Morgan hesitates near the door.

> WYATT
> Haven't you had enough? Why don't you come on back to your sweet little girl and call it a night?

> MORGAN
> You're gettin' old, Wyatt. I promised Bob one more chance to win his money back.

> WYATT
> (accepts, turns away)
> Keep your eyes open.

Morgan gives him a jaunty, dismissive wave and goes into the billiard parlor. Wyatt continues

down the sidewalk, looking around warily into the rainy darkness.

EXT. COSMOPOLITAN HOTEL—NIGHT
Wyatt walks slowly through the rain to the front entrance of the hotel. Through the door he can see another Earp friend, TEXAS JACK VERMILLION, on casual guard—he sits in a chair facing the door with a Winchester across his lap, reading a dime novel.

Wyatt hesitates, thinking, then looks back in the direction he came from. Finally, he goes back that way, looking around as he goes.

INT. CAMPBELL & HATCH SALOON AND BILLIARD PARLOR—NIGHT
Morgan is involved in a joking, serious game of pool with Bob Hatch. Sherm McMasters and some other men look on. Wyatt comes in, shaking off the rain.

> MORGAN
> Look who don't know if he's comin' or goin'. You're just in time to see me whip Bob's ass for the fiftieth time.

Wyatt takes off his hat and sits in a chair against the wall.

> BOB HATCH
> Wyatt, maybe you can answer a question that's been doggin' me for years…
> (strokes a nice shot, grins at Morgan)
> …How come Morgan is the only Earp who's completely full of shit?

WYATT
(as Morgan laughs)
Bob, the whole family wants to know the answer to that one.

Morgan has his back to the door at the rear of the billiard parlor. Suddenly one of the four glass panels in the top half of the door IMPLODES with a deafening CRASH and three GUNSHOTS. Morgan is hit square in the back and blasted forward onto the pool table. Another shot EXPLODES the wall just above Wyatt's head. There is panic, shouts, and plenty of hitting the floor in the pool hall. Wyatt and Sherm immediately have revolvers in hand and rush out the rear door, pausing only an instant to check the alley.

EXT. ALLEY ENTRANCE, END OF THE BLOCK—NIGHT
It's hard to see in the rain and darkness, but three men pass through a sliver of light as they run out of the alley and split in two directions. If you're quick, you can recognize Frank Stillwell, Pete Spence, and a Mexican known as INDIAN CHARLIE. Behind them somewhere, a SHOT is blindly fired.

EXT. ALLEY BEHIND THE BILLIARD PARLOR—NIGHT
Bob Hatch clamors out of the pool hall, cocking a shotgun just as Sherm and Wyatt move back into the light,

guns drawn, unable to see a target. In the distance, the SOUND OF HOOFBEATS. Wyatt hurries back inside.

INT. CAMPBELL & HATCH SALOON AND BILLIARD PARLOR—NIGHT
The Patrons inside have tried to make Morgan comfortable. He lies on his back on the pool table, his dark blood quickly replacing the green of the table's felt. Wyatt pushes his way to Morgan's side and leans in close. The only time we've seen this look on his face before was when Urilla died.

PATRON
We sent for the Doctor and Lou, Wyatt.

WYATT
It's going to be all right, Morg.

Bob Hatch comes back inside and turns to a thirteen-year-old BARBOY, who stands terrified in the corner.

BOB HATCH
Go find James and Virgil Earp.

The Barboy nods unconvincingly and runs out the front door. Morgan looks up at Wyatt.

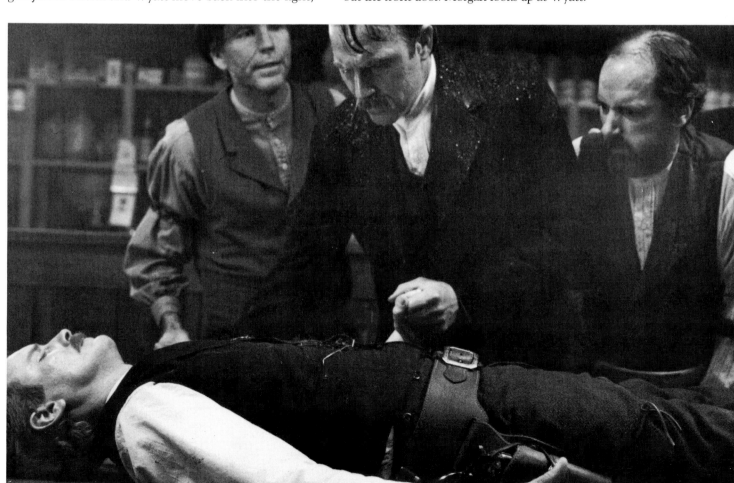

MORGAN

They got me, Wyatt. Don't let them get
you.

WYATT

You're not going to die on me, Morg.... I
won't let you.

MORGAN

Put my legs out straight.

WYATT

They are, Morg.

MORGAN
(voice fading)
It won't be long now...Where's Lou?

WYATT

She's coming.

MORGAN

Wyatt...

Wyatt puts his ear down next to Morgan's
mouth. Morgan whispers to Wyatt. Wyatt listens, then raises his head so Morgan can see
him and nods. But Morgan cannot see him. His
stare has gone blank. Now his body shakes for
one last time and he seems to exhale all the life
with one wretched rattle. He's dead.

Wyatt lifts away from his brother. He's in agony
and seems not to be quite aware of his surroundings. When the front door BANGS OPEN and
a frantic Lou rushes in, Wyatt can only watch
as she goes to the pool table and throws herself
upon her husband, WAILING. Doctor Goodfellow is close behind her, but to Wyatt the
whole scene seems to be taking place in slow
motion. He can only watch and try to understand...understand how everything that's happened has led to this dreadful moment.

EXT. TOUGH NUT STREET—NIGHT
The Barboy rounds the corner and peers franti-
cally off down the block. There are half a dozen
Pedestrians hurrying along through the rain. He
sees something and runs down there.

Virgil, limping a little from his healing leg
wound, is making his way down the block.

BARBOY

Marshal Earp, you gotta come quick! It's your
brother Morgan.

VIRGIL

What?

BARBOY

He's at Hatch's! Hurry!

The Barboy turns and runs off ahead of Virgil,
disappearing around the corner. Virgil sets off
after him, moving diagonally across the street as
fast as he can. His path takes him in front of a
half-constructed new wooden structure.

FROM INSIDE THE CONSTRUCTION
SITE we see Virgil moving along the street.
Now, three hulking SILHOUETTES rise up
with shotguns amidst the skeleton of the building. All three weapons hone in on Virgil and
proceed to BLAST AWAY. Virgil is hit on the
left side, taking at least one direct hit on his arm,
shattering it. He flies into the mud. Beyond him,
a hapless horse is sprayed in the flanks with buck-
shot and goes down writhing in a puddle. Windows across the street from the construction site
SHATTER.

EXT. FIFTH STREET—NIGHT
AROUND THE CORNER the Barboy has slid
to a confused stop, hearing the uproar behind
him. He turns, terrified, and starts back that
way. He's almost to the alley when he hears
HOOFBEATS coming across his path and
jumps into the shadows.

From out of the alley ride three Horseman, one
still desperately trying to get mounted. Even in
the rain and the hubbub, we can make out Ike
Clanton, Curly Bill and Johnny Ringo. Ike is
the one having trouble mounting. He finally
gets up on the moving horse, but loses his hat
in the mud. The three men gallop off into the
darkness.

The Barboy, crying and trembling, comes forward. He looks after the men, then bends and
picks up Ike's lost hat.

"WHY DOES IT ALWAYS HAVE TO BE THE DAMN BROTHERS?"

W hen you read any story or history of Wyatt Earp, you realize that keeping a family was terribly important to him. That's really the story. If you're gonna do a story about the man, you can do a story about the OK Corral, but you realize that what led up to most of the events in his life was the fact that he was very strong about keeping the family together."   —KEVIN COSTNER

O ur father, Nicholas, instilled a lot of ideas in us about how to handle ourselves out in the world. He taught us to have a lot of respect for the family, that it was the most important thing, always. I think that we all had that idea anyway. His telling us that wouldn't necessarily have made us be that way unless we had it in us. I think we got a lot from Pop. I think he told us the way things should be, and he was an example. And we lived by his example. We grew up and, in one

way, it's an American classic, and in another way, it's an American tragedy. Depends on how you look at it. Because of the sacrifices that the Earps had to make for their lifestyle, a lot of bad things happened. They're a very interesting family.

"The family ran a faro game in Tombstone, the Earps owned part of a saloon. But Virgil's not really a game-player or gambling man. I think he was a little more interested in a traditional way of life without too much extraneous activity. He went on to become marshal of another town years after he recovered from his wounds, after he was ambushed in Tombstone. Then he went to pan for gold. He went mining in Nevada. And his wife went with him. He died of pneumonia in 1907. His wife, Allie, wrote a book about them.

"Virgil, or any one of them, could have done it alone, but they had a couple of brothers, so why not bring them in. I think that's why the story has been told so many times and that's why they made the mark that they did. That's why they're so remembered—because of their power of being together. They backed each other up. I don't find Virgil or Wyatt or Morgan or any of us to be that far away from who I am as a man or who I might have been if I had lived back then. I understand where they're all coming from. I don't think Larry would have cast me in the film if he didn't know that I understood what he was trying to do."
          —MICHAEL MADSEN (VIRGIL)

M organ did a lot of different things. He was a part-time deputy, whenever his brothers needed a deputy. He rode shotgun for Wells Fargo. He was a gambler, a faro dealer, a bartender. He did whatever the family needed him to do.

"The guy likes to have fun. I think he was a troublemaker. He's the wrong guy to bring to the gunfight if you wanted anything besides a gunfight. Virgil is steady. He's the mediator, the ambassador. Wyatt is a hard-liner but he wants to do what's right, for the family. James is into his own thing. And Morgan is the catalyst. He's a wild child. You've got all these semi-stable components and then you throw Morgan in and it blows up. He's

Virgil Earp

Morgan Earp

140

the fun-loving one. He's hot-tempered and maybe a little crazy, but at the same time very gentle, very loving. I mean, you look at his relationship with his as-good-as wife, Lou, and you see that it was different from his brothers' relationships. It was very loving and tender."

—LINDEN ASHBY (MORGAN)

James was the eldest son; he went to the Civil War and fought for the Union. At the begining of the movie, he comes back barely alive. And I think as a result of his experiences there, he never really took on the patriarchal role that an older brother might have been expected to.

"He was a gambler and a saloon man. That's how he made his living. James didn't partake in the gunplay that all his brothers did, for a number of reasons, I think. First, he came back from the Civil War pretty messed up. He had taken a .53 caliber slug to the shoulder, which left him somewhat crippled. I think he walked out of that with something. As opposed to being damaged by it, I like to think that James walked out with something positive, which was the sense that what life was really about was living. That's different from the other brothers, and it's different from what his father had given him. Nicholas instilled in the family this great sense of responsibility and duty. But I think James saw the horrors of the Civil War, which was a really gruesome, gory thing to go through, and saw the insanity in what [his father's] strict code could lead to. I think it made him want to enjoy his life.

He was an alcoholic, but I think it's difficult to judge his alcoholism from a 1990s perspective, because, back then, most people were drunks. And he was definitely very functional. He lived to be older than Wyatt. He died a little earlier, but he had lived longer.

"Another very interesting thing about James is that he was married to a working prostitute, and he made no bones about it. That's a pretty far-out guy for the 1800s. He didn't make any apologies for it. He didn't think any less of his wife for doing that. So I think he was pretty advanced for his time."

—DAVID ANDREWS (JAMES)

David Andrews as James Earp (above) and James Caviezel as Warren Earp (below)

"Kill 'em all."

INT. VIRGIL'S ROOM, COSMOPOLITAN HOTEL—NIGHT
Virgil is being treated on his bed and it's a bloody mess. Dr. Goodfellow directs two Assistants and Bessie Earp in the operation. While Virgil has taken a superficial hit in his side, he may have been saved by his left arm. That's where Good-fellow is concentrating his efforts as Allie, in shock from the combined events of the evening, clings tightly to Virgil's good hand. Virgil presents Allie with a brave smile. Wyatt comes in.

> WYATT
> How is he?

> ALLIE
> (coldly)
> You can see for yourself.

> VIRGIL
> (pleading)
> Wyatt, don't let him take my arm. He wants to cut it off.

> WYATT
> You heard him, Doc.

> DR. GOODFELLOW
> Either way, he's gonna be a cripple…if he doesn't bleed to death.

> VIRGIL
> At least I'll be a two-armed corpse.

Allie breaks down in tears.

> VIRGIL
> Never mind, I've got one arm left to hug you with.

Allie tries to manage a smile. Virgil looks beyond the crowd of moving bodies through the open door to the next room.

> VIRGIL
> Where's Morgan?

Allie lowers her eyes and begins to sob. Virgil is in the dark.

INT. HALLWAY, COSMOPOLITAN HOTEL—NIGHT
Wyatt steps out into the hall and seems to take his first breath in a while. He crosses to a door down the hall and quietly opens it.

Doc sits on the steps, his back against the wall. He's drinking from a flask and his eyes are redder than normal. In his hand is Ike Clanton's lost, muddy hat. Doc hands it to Wyatt, who looks at it without surprise, then drops it on the floor. Wyatt makes no move to close the curtain.

> DOC
> I'm so sorry, Wyatt…
> (his voice cracks)
> …I loved that boy like he was my own stupid little brother…

Doc is crying now, tears rolling down his cheeks. He tries to sniff it clear, but that only provokes a violent coughing fit. Finally, handkerchief to mouth, he is able to get under control.

> DOC
> What do you want to do?

CLOSE ON WYATT, looking out into the night. He looks different than we have ever seen him. Something decent in him has died. And something dark and hard and implacable has replaced it.

> WYATT
> Kill 'em all.

EXT. WELLS FARGO DEPOT—DAY
The stagecoach has recently arrived and disgorged its passengers. One of them, a handsome young man of 26 with unmistakable bloodlines, carries his satchel away from the depot, asking directions once.

EXT. COSMOPOLITAN HOTEL—DAY
The place is still heavily fortified; armed Earp Allies protect the entrance. The young man approaches the hotel, but is stopped by TURKEY CREEK JACK JOHNSON. They are engaged in a discussion when Wyatt happens out the front door. When he sees the young man, he moves to him and embraces him. It is his youngest brother, WARREN EARP.

> WARREN
> I've come to help bring Morgan home to Ma and Pa.

> WYATT
> I'm glad you're here, Warren.

INT. LOU'S ROOM—NIGHT
Josie sits quietly next to the bed in the gloomy room. Lou lies on her stomach, head in a pillow, softly keening. Josie indicates to Wyatt that there's nothing more for him, or anyone, to do here.

INT. HALLWAY—NIGHT
Wyatt comes out of Lou's room and wanders down the hall to the stairwell. Curtains cover the window there, but Wyatt pushes them open a ways and stares out into the darkness.

> DOC (OS)
> Careful…I don't want them taking a shot at you.

INT. MATTIE'S ROOM—DAY

Mattie sits on the edge of the bed staring at the wall; she's half-dressed. There is a partially packed trunk on the floor and clothes strewn about. Wyatt comes in.

> WYATT
> It's time to go now, Mattie.

She looks up at him, very stoned.

> MATTIE
> Sure, sugar. Off to California with the Earps…
> (gives him a strange smile)
> Hmm. You're the only brother who hasn't been shot. That's not fair…

She lifts a gun from her side, points it at his head. He ducks as she FIRES.

INT. HALLWAY—DAY

Warren and Sherm McMasters come running down the hall, guns drawn. Wyatt opens the door to Mattie's room from the inside. Mattie lies on the bed, sobbing. He hands Warren the revolver Mattie used.

> WYATT
> There was an accident. Everything's okay now.

He closes the door on the two men.

INT. MATTIE'S ROOM—DAY

Wyatt sits on the bed.

> WYATT
> Mattie, if you want to go on the train with the others, you'll have to go now. I don't know when I'll be back here.

> MATTIE
> Go to hell. When you get back, I'll be gone.

She sits up woozily and snatches a bottle of laudanum from the table. Wyatt makes no attempt to stop her from taking a pull.

> WYATT
> If you keep up with that stuff, it'll kill you.

> MATTIE
> What do you care?

Wyatt looks at her, then finally gets up.

> WYATT
> I don't anymore.

EXT. TRAIN DEPOT, CONTENTION, ARIZONA—DAY

Two buckboard wagons are pulled up next to the growling train. One wagon has been full of luggage; the other has carried Morgan's coffin and various crates containing the easily transportable possessions of the Earp Clan as they pull up stakes from Tombstone. The able-bodied men in the traveling party—Wyatt, Doc, Warren, Sherm—help Train Porters place Morgan's coffin in the baggage car and turn to the rest of the luggage.

DOWN THE TRAIN. James and Allie supervise as Virgil, hobbled and heavily bandaged but ambulatory, is helped up to a train compartment by the Train Porters. Bessie, who seemed so rough with Lou back in Tombstone, now tenderly guides the still dazed young widow up into the passenger car.

The Station Master comes down the track with a telegram in hand and gives it to Doc. Wyatt and Warren watch him read it.

> DOC
> It's from Bob Paul in Tucson. He says Ike Clanton, Frank Stillwell and some of their friends are in Tucson and they've been watching the trains. Seems like someone in Tombstone told them we were coming.

> WYATT
> Good.
> (turns to Warren)
> We'll go as far as Tucson and get you out of the territory. You'll stay on the train and help James and the women get Virgil and Morg home to California.

> WARREN
> (shakes his head "no")
> James and them can get Morgan back. If you're going after the men that did this, I'm going with you.

Wyatt gives him a look. He's as headstrong as Morgan was.

LATER. The train huffs its way out of the station and into the desert.

EXT. DESERT—MAGIC HOUR
The train shoots black smoke into the red sky as the sun sinks beneath the desert horizon.

INT. EARPS' CAR—NIGHT
The train is slowing for its arrival in Tucson. This car is entirely filled with the Earp party. A Conductor helps Wyatt turn down the lamps in the car as the others pull all the shades. Wyatt motions Warren up to the front of the car.

> WYATT
> James'll watch the back door, you watch this one. Anybody tries to come on, shoot 'em.

EXT. EARPS' CAR, RAIL YARD, TUCSON—NIGHT
The train is still slowing down as Wyatt, Doc and Sherm drop off onto the ground. Wyatt carries a shotgun, Sherm a Winchester, and Doc his nickel-plated revolver.

Wyatt begins walking stealthily down one side of the train toward the station, Doc and Sherm down the other.

EXT. TRACKS NEAR DEPOT, TUCSON—NIGHT
Ike Clanton, Frank Stillwell, and Johnny Ringo, all armed, appear from between two railroad cars. They look up the tracks at the approaching train, murmur to each other and split up, Stillwell going in one direction, Clanton and Ringo off in another.

Doc and Sherm come down the tracks, peering about. They speak, then split off in two directions in the darkness.

Wyatt walks carefully down the tracks as the train he just left comes to a halt in the station. Wyatt bends as he walks to look under the other trains waiting in the yard and checks between cars at the couplings. Suddenly, sensing something, he stops, waits, listens. Then, like a cat, he disappears under one of the stationary cars.

ON THE ROOF OF A FREIGHT CAR. Ringo climbs up, then settles himself in a prone position from which he has a vantage on the tracks and depot. He sights along the newly arrived train to the passenger cars, one of which is the darkened Earp car.

ON A LOADING DOCK. Ike hops up onto the dock and settles himself and his Winchester in the shadows with a clear view of the depot platform and into the passenger cars if the train pulls out. He tenses as he sees Sherm come into the light of the platform, mingling with the regular Passengers, looking around.

ON THE TRACKS. Frank Stillwell, revolver in hand, moves along behind a train sitting on the track parallel to the Earp train. He climbs up onto the platform between two cars and looks over at the Earp train's passenger cars.

STILLWELL'S POV as he looks down the line of passenger cars. As his eye reaches the darkened car, Warren appears for a moment out of the shadows of the doorway cradling a Winchester, then disappears back into the car.

Stillwell, encouraged now, hops back down on the far side of his train, about to move up the line closer to the Earp car. He's just landed

when he looks up and GASPS. Wyatt stands silhouetted six feet away, his shotgun raised at Stillwell. Stillwell has his gun in his hand, but he remains frozen in terror.

> WYATT
> You murdered my brother.

Stillwell raises his hand, as if to ward off the coming onslaught. He seems almost unaware that it is the hand that holds his Colt.

> STILLWELL
> No!

Wyatt fires one barrel of the shotgun into Stillwell's gut. He is blown back into the gravel. Wyatt steps forward over the prone body, his look horrible.

> WYATT
> Yes.

He points the shotgun down at Stillwell and fires the other barrel.

ON THE LOADING DOCK Ike flinches at the second blast. He shrinks back.

ON THE ROOF OF THE FREIGHT CAR Ringo shifts his body around, trying to locate the source of the shots. It's hidden from his view.

BETWEEN TRAINS Doc has been stalking, searching fruitlessly. But now he sees the flash of Ringo's Winchester on the roof of the freight car. Doc steadies his arm and fires a shot in that direction.

Ringo is shocked by a near miss on the rooftop, not sure where it came from. He rolls in the opposite direction and barely stops himself from falling to the tracks. As it is, he looks like a frightened monkey as he half-falls, half-scrambles down the ladder on the opposite side and runs off into the darkness.

Wyatt hears nothing, or cares not at all. He is standing over Stillwell's body with a crazed look on his face. He takes out his Colt and *fires it down toward the lifeless body*. As he is firing away, Sherm appears at a run. Wyatt raises his gun momentarily at the newcomer, recognizes Sherm and lowers his gun again to fire until empty.

"Kill 'em all."

I n this sequence I think Wyatt steps out of himself. It's no longer about the OK Corral. The OK Corral was over for him. He also probably knew that people were on the hunt for him, to take him out the way they took his brothers out. When those cowboys killed Morgan and shot Virgil, they had no idea that Wyatt would put down his badge for over a year and hunt them down. It's terrifying, really. And these guys were dying with bullets in their fronts. These guys weren't getting waylaid. These guys were being hunted down and they were looking at him when he killed them."
—KEVIN COSTNER

I think the loss of Morgan is one of the large tragedies in Wyatt's life and he feels some guilt about it. He feels that somehow his management of the situation from just before the gunfight at the OK Corral through the aftermath has somehow led to his brother's death. And that guilt fuels his revenge, which probably would have been intense anyway. There's the added weight that, perhaps, he had something to do with it. He is on a blood rampage. It's the final extension of his code. It actually plays into one of his deepest beliefs, which is that his family is the most important thing and that if one of them is threatened, the others must step forward. When one of them is killed, the others must revenge. In some ways he's very simple and rigid, and that causes a lot of problems."
—LAWRENCE KASDAN

ON THE LOADING DOCK these GUN-SHOTS are too much for Ike; too easily can he conjure up the scene of what's happening. He pulls his Winchester to his body and runs off in the other direction.

Back on the tracks, Doc has arrived at Wyatt's position. He looks with amazement at the body on the ground, then up at Wyatt's face, as if seeing it for the first time. He puts a gentle hand on Wyatt.

> DOC
> Okay, Wyatt…let's go.

They turn away from the mutilated corpse and find Warren up on the platform between the cars of the empty train. It's impossible to know how much he's seen, but from the horror in his eyes it's clear he's never seen anything like it before. He looks at Wyatt, dumbstruck.

INT. EARPS' CAR—NIGHT
The train is starting to crawl out of the station. Good-byes have already been said. Sherm and Doc are down on the platform with their things. Warren gives a final wave to the remaining

Earps and hops off. Wyatt stops at the injured Virgil on his way to the door.

> WYATT
> It's all right, Virg. One for Morg.

Virgil acknowledges it with sadness. Wyatt touches his shoulder and goes out the door, hopping off the train onto the platform. Virgil and Allie (who's crying), James and Bessie, and the shell-shocked Lou look grimly forward as the train heads off to California.

EXT. COSMOPOLITAN HOTEL, TOMBSTONE—DAY
Wyatt, Warren, Sherm and Doc ride up, tired and dust-covered from their return trip. A telegraph operator named ALBERT hurries up to Wyatt with a telegram in his hand.

> ALBERT
> Marshal Earp, I think you ought to take a look at this. I haven't showed it to Sheriff Behan yet…
> (a beat, shy)
> Your brother was a good man.

INT. JOSIE'S ROOM, COSMOPOLITAN HOTEL—DAY
Josie enfolds the dusty Wyatt in a passionate embrace. Wyatt holds her face close as he speaks to her.

> WYATT
> I want you to go home to your folks in San Francisco. When I can, I'll come and get you.

> JOSIE
> When will that be?

> WYATT
> I have some men I have to see. I don't know where that will take me.

Josie holds him, as if for dear life.

> JOSIE
> I'll be expecting you every day.

> WYATT
> I'm broke, you know that.

> JOSIE
> It doesn't matter.

> WYATT
> I swear, Josie, we made money here. Not a lot, but we made money.

> JOSIE
> Then there's nothing left to hold you.

> WYATT
> There's my…I was gonna say my family.

> JOSIE
> I'll be your family, Wyatt. I'll give you children…we'll make our own place where no one will ever find us…and I won't die on you. I swear it.

> WYATT
> You were right, Josie. We stayed too long.

EXT. COSMOPOLITAN HOTEL—DAY
There is a buckboard in front loaded with bedrolls, bags and supplies; Texas Jack is wrangling it. Sherm, Doc, Warren, Turkey Creek Jack, and Wyatt are just preparing to mount up. John Clum, looking distraught, is talking to Wyatt.

Wyatt hands it back to him and gives him an appreciative look.

> WYATT
> I'm grateful, Albert.
> (to the others)
> They got a warrant out for us on Stillwell already. I guess everybody in Tucson saw us there.

> DOC
> Really? Even with you bein' so quiet and all?

> WYATT
> We better collect our stuff and go. Sherm, see if the two Jacks will take a ride with us.

> WARREN
> (confused)
> Wyatt, you're still a marshal here, ain't you?

> DOC
> Sure, but now he's gonna be a marshal *and* an outlaw…
> (heading inside)
> …the best of both worlds, son.

152

CLUM
You couldn't have been trying to arrest him, Wyatt, not with close to twenty bullet holes in his body.

WYATT
No, I wasn't trying to arrest him.

CLUM
(disturbed by his friend)
I…I don't know what to say to that…

Wyatt hands him an envelope.

WYATT
This is my will, John. I've named you as executor. Not that there's much left…

CLUM
This is not a jungle, Wyatt. We have laws.

WYATT
Yes, we do. And if these men think they can hide behind those laws…then they have missed their guess.

Johnny Behan hurries down the street with three heavily armed (but nervous) Deputies in tow. Behan has the telegram we've seen earlier in his hand. Passing Townspeople stop to watch the confrontation.

BEHAN
Wyatt, I want to see you.

Wyatt swings up onto his horse, then speaks down at Behan, like ice.

WYATT
Johnny, if you're not careful, you'll see me once too often.

Wyatt sweeps a dismissive glance over the Deputies as he wheels his horse and leads his group out.

EXT. ALLEN STREET—DAY
Wyatt and his posse ride down the busy street. Wyatt looks at the town with a kind of wistfulness. This is the end for him. He may never ride this street again. His dreams for the family here are in ashes.

EXT. DESERT/MOUNTAIN FOOTHILLS—DAY
SERIES OF SHOTS. Wyatt's posse leaves its supply buckboard behind and heads up into the foothills of the Dragoon Mountains.

EXT. MINING EXCHANGE, FREMONT STREET, TOMBSTONE—DAY
Johnny Behan stands on the sidewalk speaking to an as yet unseen group of horsemen, the Behan Posse.

                    BEHAN
        ...and by that duly constituted power do
        hereby name each of you a Temporary
        Deputy Sheriff of Cochise County, with
        all the rights and authority that entails.
        Let's get going.

We see the Behan Posse, assembled on horseback before Johnny: It is 20 men strong, a half dozen regular Deputies, the rest clearly Cowboys and rough Rustler types. As they swing away to leave town, we see prominent among them Ike Clanton and Billy Claiborne.

EXT. PETE SPENCE'S WOODCAMP, DRAGOON MOUNTAINS—DAY
A half dozen Woodchoppers, mostly Mexican, move about among the three dilapidated buildings of the camp, hauling loads of wood and tending to the work. One by one now, they notice something in the distance and stop to watch, with some trepidation.

WHAT THEY SEE. Three riders: Warren, Sherm, and Turkey Creek Jack are working their way down the entry trail on the opposite hill.

Indian Charlie, whom we saw running away from Morgan's murder, comes out of one of the buildings, buckling on his holster. When he sees the approaching riders, he ducks quickly back inside, grabs a Winchester and ducks out the back door.

The three riders come into the camp. They take in everything, but their manner is casual. The MEXICAN FOREMAN comes forward.

                    SHERM
        We're looking for Pete Spence.

                    FOREMAN
        He no here.

                    SHERM
        This is his camp, ain't it?

                    FOREMAN
            (nods)
        He no here. He go to Tombstone.

                    WARREN
        Tombstone?

                    SHERM
        How 'bout the one they call Indian
        Charlie?

The Foreman reacts quizzically, making a show of not recognizing the name. We SMASH CUT TO:

EXT. WOODS NEAR WOODCAMP—DAY
Violent movement. Indian Charlie crashes through the underbrush among the trees. He's sweating, terrified, frantic. He looks over his shoulder, through the foliage. Behind him, Doc Holliday, on horseback, is riding at the periphery of the stand of trees. Now Doc fires a SHOT into the woods. Indian Charlie turns, fires one SHOT from his Winchester, then moves desperately onward.

EXT. CLEARING, WOODS NEAR WOODCAMP—DAY
Indian Charlie breaks out of the stand of trees and skids to a stop. Thirty feet away, Wyatt sits on his lathered, snorting horse. His Colt is in his hand.

Indian Charlie is terrified. He spreads his arms submissively and throws the Winchester away. Wyatt's look does not soften. He slides off his horse and walks toward Indian Charlie. When he is ten feet from him, Wyatt stops and holsters his Colt. He stands waiting to draw.

Indian Charlie takes a moment to understand what is happening. When he does, he wants

nothing to do with it. Terrified, he shakes his head "no" vigorously.

Wyatt looks at him with dead eyes.

Indian Charlie hears the noisy approach of Doc through the woods. He doesn't know what to do, but he knows he has to do it now. He draws his revolver.

Wyatt is quicker. His first shot catches Indian Charlie in the head. He shoots him three more times before the body has settled.

Doc comes into the clearing on his horse. He stops. Looks.

>   DOC
>   (quietly, to himself)
>   I was supposed to be the crazy one.

EXT. CANYON, FOOTHILLS OF THE DRAGOON MOUNTAINS—DAY
Behan's Posse, their score of horses raising a hellacious cloud of dust, rides through a canyon pass.

HIGH ABOVE THEM Wyatt and Doc are prone on a boulder, looking at the show below. Off behind them, on the flat ground up here, is the rest of the Earp Posse, holding their horses quiet. Texas Jack and his supply buckboard is here too.

Doc gives Wyatt a concerned look, but Wyatt is unresponsive, rising up and heading back to the group. Doc watches him go, unhappy. He feels a coughing fit coming on and quickly covers his mouth with his handkerchief to stifle the sound.

EXT. CAMPSITE, WHETSTONE MOUN-TAINS—NIGHT
The Earp Posse is camped for the night. Wyatt leaves the others around the fire and comes over to where Doc is sitting alone, drinking from his flask. Wyatt settles near him.

>   WYATT
>   Something bothering you?

>   DOC
>   What makes you so sure Curly Bill is
>   with this pack we're trailing now?

>   WYATT
>   (he's not sure)
>   That's what Texas Jack's friend told him.

>   DOC
>   Maybe he's wrong. Maybe it's just a
>   bunch of ordinary rustlers out about their
>   business. Are you going to shoot all of
>   them too?

Wyatt settles back against a rock, weary.

THE ART OF GUNSHOT WOUNDS

O ur job is to hide the explosive in the blood pack and make it look real, as real as we can. You're adding almost a half an inch of girth to a human body and it can only be shot certain ways. Usually you've got to shoot it head-on. We try to disguise the piece to the point where you can't tell. That's the whole object. You pick an area of the body that's going to be seen on camera. You take a cast of that, create a positive form in stone, and then you apply the plate that protects the actor from the explosive. You apply the explosive. You apply the blood bag to the stone positive, and then you sculpt over that, and you create a negative mold that would house all that. Then you inject the foam latex inside this space and you bake it and it turns to rubber. Then you have a piece, a duplicate of the body part, and on the back of it there'd be a reservoir, cast in the form, to house the blood bag, the explosive and the metal plate. You go ahead and glue that into position and the rest of it is up to the art of it. You blend the piece into the skin and paint it to look real for the camera."

—MIKE MILLS, MAKE-UP DEPARTMENT HEAD

The Make-up Department makes the appliance. They do all the live castings on the actor and make the latex appliance. They work with us on the quantity of blood, the size of pyrotechnic charge that we can put between the appliance and the person's skin, what kind of protective vacuum we can use, and how much we can get away with, so we can get the desired effect. We work directly with them in painting the protection piece underneath a red color so it shows as red, or blood. Either they or us make the blood bag that goes inside the appliance. We're actually doing the charge that blows through it. We're the ones who actually fire the button and generally get either the glory or the lawsuits. We'll always supply the squib [or explosive] and the wire, and then we'll either detonate it or let the actor detonate it himself with a hit box he carries on his body. What we prefer to do is hard-wire it right to us so we have total control over it and we can decide when it goes off and not leave it up to the actor, so he doesn't have to worry about his lines, hitting his marks, and pushing the button.

"It simplifies it greatly [when the hit is in the clothes rather than on the skin] because you don't have to color match and make-up match all the appliance pieces. It's much easier to protect the actor with padding and much easier to reset. You can just change the clothes, and once you know what it's going to be, you can do numerous takes. You're ready to go. You can speed it up. If you need it to be grosser, you can add anything, whatever you have on hand. Some people have gotten as gross as adding chicken guts, or more reliable, easier things, such as tissue paper or anything you've got on your shelf. Oatmeal, anything like that, anything that will read 'disgusting.'" —BURT DALTON, SPECIAL EFFECTS COORDINATOR

WYATT

You're free to take off any time you want.

DOC

Go to hell. That's a nice way to talk to
me.
        (looks at him)
You can't get what you want, Wyatt. You
can't kill them all. Hell, Ike Clanton and
Johnny Ringo are riding with Behan.
They're as much lawmen as you are right
now. And there's too many of them for
us to take.
        (after a moment)
Look, I'm dead anyway. So if you want to
go out in a blaze of glory, I'm with you.
But if you want to live…

WYATT

What do you want me to do…forget
about it?

DOC
        ("no")
Just wait. Get out of Arizona for a while.
Make 'em think it's over. We'll come
back later and pick 'em off one at a time.

Doc begins to cough, violently. It seems to be
getting worse. Wyatt watches as Doc tries to get

control. He's wondering how long Doc has to
come back anywhere.

WYATT

You need to go to Colorado…one of
those sanitariums in the mountains.

Doc looks up from his handkerchief. He nods at
Wyatt.

DOC

I'll go…if you'll take me.

Wyatt looks at him a long time.

WYATT

You've been a good friend to me, Doc.

DOC
        (after a beat)
Shut up.

EXT. MESCAL SPRING, WHETSTONE
MOUNTAINS—DAY

Wyatt is in the lead as his group comes though
a narrow space into the wider flat that borders
the Spring. Wyatt dismounts as the others trail
single file into the Spring area.

Suddenly, nine Cowboys (Curly Bill, Johnny
Ringo and Pete Spence among them) rise from
hidden positions in the rocks and open fire.
Curly Bill is closest to Wyatt and concentrates
his fire on him. The Earp Posse members draw
their weapons and fire from horseback, quite
reasonably wheeling their horses to head back
toward the relative cover of the trail. (Turkey
Creek Jack's horse is shot out from under him,
and he jumps up behind Sherm to retreat.)
Doc, however, rides forward, firing away to pro-
vide cover for Wyatt. He shoots Johnny Ringo,
who falls dead from a high rock. Wyatt hits
Pete Spence, killing him.

DOC

C'mon, Wyatt, let's go!

But Wyatt will not go. Doc retreats. Wyatt pulls
his shotgun from the scabbard on his wildly
shying horse. A moment later, the saddle horn
is blown completely off by a blast from the Cowboys. Wyatt seems not to care. His long over-
coat is actually shredded by three shots as he
raises the shotgun, very deliberately, at Curly
Bill.

Curly Bill, who has been firing away with his Winchester at what now appears to be an invulnerable Wyatt, has a split-second of terror before Wyatt fires both barrels at him. Curly Bill is blown almost in half.

The sight has a catalyzing effect on both sides. The Cowboys are shocked and shaken by the presence of this seemingly inhuman killing machine. Still firing, they abandon their positions and head for their mounts. The Earp Posse rides back into the open space, firing away. Doc rides up toward Wyatt and pulls up; *we LINGER ON Doc's face as he looks down at Wyatt.*

Wyatt lowers his shotgun. The SOUNDS of the scene, GUNSHOTS, HORSES, SHOUTS, begin to FADE AWAY. Wyatt looks off at the remains of Curly Bill. Wyatt is somewhere else.

DISSOLVE TO:

EXT. STEAMSHIP, COAST OF ALASKA (1898)—DAY
Magnificent mountains. Green slopes blanketed with evergreens. Vistas so wide and deep they dwarf the wonders of the lower forty-eight. If you were looking for somewhere to go when the West ran out of room, this would be the place.

The S.S. *City of Seattle* plows the waters of the Gulf of Alaska. The Great Gold Rush is on and the decks are packed to capacity with crazy, hopeful, foolish Seekers after fortune. Every inch that isn't occupied by a body is crammed with someone's supplies. At the rail, admiring the incredible views of the coast, two more Seekers—

Wyatt, fifty years old, and Josie, thirty-eight, look across the water. She takes his arm, but the girlishness is missing now. There's a maturity and stamina to this union now. And they know what tickles the other one.

JOSIE

Show me where our gold is, Wyatt. Point it out.

He gives her a sidelong glance, then goes along. Slowly he lifts his arm and points.

JOSIE

Right there? Well, that doesn't look so tough.

WYATT

No, I imagine we can pick most of it up with just a day's excursion out of Nome. The problem will be lugging it back to town.

JOSIE
(accepts that deadpan)
And what are we going to do with all our money?

Wyatt seems genuinely stymied by this question. He's been chasing it his whole life without much thought. Like a lot of us.

JOSIE

We'll buy you a new suit. You could use one.

A YOUNG MAN has made a hesitant trip across the deck to reach them and hovered nearby. Now he approaches. He's wearing the rough clothes he imagines a prospector would wear.

YOUNG MAN
Excuse me. I'm sorry to bother…

Wyatt and Josie turn to him.

YOUNG MAN
I'm sorry, but are you, by any chance, Wyatt Earp?

Wyatt nods. The Young Man is very excited. He offers his hand and shakes Wyatt's vigorously.

YOUNG MAN
My name's Francis O'Rourke. I believe you saved my uncle's life one time…in Tombstone, Arizona. That's the story my father told us, anyway. Many times, believe me.

Wyatt is not sure what he's referring to.

WYATT
This is my wife, Josie.

YOUNG MAN
It's an honor, ma'am.

JOSIE
I'm afraid my husband saved so many lives…
(Wyatt shoots her a disapproving look)
…he can't keep track of them all.

YOUNG MAN
Oh, you'd remember this—if the story's true. My uncle's name was Tommy O'Rourke, but they called him Tommy Behind-the-Deuce.

Both Wyatt and Josie react to this with smiles of recognition.

YOUNG MAN

I thought so. So I guess my father's story is true. He said my uncle killed a mining man named Schneider in a card game. And this Schneider fellow was very popular and pretty soon a lynch mob had formed…

EXT. ALLEN STREET, TOMBSTONE (1880)—NIGHT

Start on the feet, many wearing miner's boots, then up to the angry faces of a Mob of fifty men marching toward us down Allen Street. Half carry rifles or shotguns, the rest shovels, clubs, and torches.

YOUNG MAN (VO)

…and was comin' down to the jail to take Tommy out and string him up.

INT. CITY JAIL—NIGHT

CLOSE ON the terrified face of TOMMY

BEHIND-THE-DEUCE, a slight, disreputable, tinhorn gambler. He's been looking out the tiny window of his cell and now turns in a panic to shout out to the front room of the jail—

TOMMY

Marshal Earp! Give me a gun…in the name of God let me protect myself!

CAMERA IS MOVING now up past a door to the front room of the jail, where Wyatt checks the cylinder of a second Colt, which he sticks in his belt along with his regular holstered .45.

WYATT
(over his shoulder)

Tommy, if I hear one more sound out of you, I'm going to help them do it.

He picks up a shotgun from the desk and goes toward the front door.

YOUG MAN (VO)
It seems your brothers were off somewhere collecting some renegade Indians in another town and you were all alone…

EXT. CITY JAIL—NIGHT
CAMERA IS STILL MOVING with Wyatt as he comes outside and stations himself on the sidewalk in front of the door. The Mob is moving down the street toward him. When they reach the front of the jail they fan out around Wyatt in a semi-circle, shouting for the prisoner.

YOUNG MAN (VO)
They were shouting that they ought to just shoot you and take Tommy. And finally, when they quieted down, you said—

WYATT
You boys can get me…that won't be any problem with all the guns you got here…
(focusing on the men in front)
…but I'm taking ten or twelve of you with me. Starting with you, Dick Gird…and you, McGee…and maybe you too, Harvey.

The men in front begin to lose their resolve.

WYATT
(louder)
So if any of you want Tommy…and you want me, then come up front with these brave men…and we'll all go together.

Dick Gird and McGee and Harvey turn away and start a slow reverse of the Mob down the street.

EXT. DECK OF STEAMSHIP (1898)—DAY
The Young Man studies Wyatt's face as he finishes his story.

YOUNG MAN
Anyway, that's what my father told us.

WYATT
What happened to your uncle?

YOUNG MAN
(a funny look)
He was shot dead up at Omaha in '87.

Josie makes a doleful face, but has to fight a smile.

YOUNG MAN
(to Wyatt)
Guess he wasn't worth savin'.

Wyatt's look suggests this is not his only dubious skirmish, but he smiles as the Young Man bows awkwardly away—

YOUNG MAN
Anyway…it's an honor, Mr. Earp…sir.

Wyatt and Josie turn to look at Alaska once again. They are silent for a while. Finally—

WYATT
Some people say it didn't happen that way.

We're behind them now, as Josie puts her hand on his.

JOSIE
Never mind them, Wyatt. It happened that way.

THE END

WARNER BROS. PRESENTS
A TIG PRODUCTIONS/KASDAN PICTURES PRODUCTION
A LAWRENCE KASDAN FILM

KEVIN COSTNER
DENNIS QUAID
GENE HACKMAN

Wyatt Earp

David Andrews · Linden Ashby · Jeff Fahey
Joanna Going · Mark Harmon · Michael Madsen
Catherine O'Hara · Bill Pullman · Isabella Rossellini
Tom Sizemore · JoBeth Williams · Mare Winningham
James Gammon · Rex Linn · Randle Mell · Adam Baldwin
Annabeth Gish · Lewis Smith · Ian Bohen · Betty Buckley
Alison Elliot · Todd Allen · MacKenzie Astin · James Caviezel
Karen Grassle · John Denis Johnston · Tea Leoni
MUSIC BY James Newton Howard
EDITED BY Carol Littleton A.C.E
PRODUCTION DESIGNER Ida Random
DIRECTOR OF PHOTOGRAPHY Owen Roizman A.S.C.
EXECUTIVE PRODUCERS
Jon Slan · Dan Gordon · Charles Okun · Michael Grillo
WRITTEN BY Dan Gordon and Lawrence Kasdan
PRODUCED BY Jim Wilson · Kevin Costner · Lawrence Kasdan
DIRECTED BY Lawrence Kasdan

ABOUT THE AUTHORS

LAWRENCE KASDAN has lived in Los Angeles for twenty years, and has been making films for much of that time. His credits as a writer-director include *Body Heat, The Big Chill, Silverado* (co-written with his brother Mark), *The Accidental Tourist* and *Grand Canyon* (co-written with his wife Meg). *Silverado* marked his first major collaboration with Kevin Costner. The two have remained close friends since that film, but did not work together again until *The Bodyguard,* which Kasdan wrote and produced with Jim Wilson and Costner. Kasdan's other writing credits include *The Empire Strikes Back, Return of the Jedi* and *Raiders of the Lost Ark.* As *Wyatt Earp* opens, Kasdan is preparing to direct a new film, *Paris Match.*

JAKE KASDAN was present through the entire production, from the earliest stages of preproduction to the recording of the musical score, serving as the film's documentarian. He compiled and edited this text, and conducted most of the interviews used. After concluding his *Wyatt Earp*-related projects, Kasdan will return to the University of California in Santa Cruz, or something.

BEN GLASS, photographer and actor, began his career photographing *Dances with Wolves.* Since that time, he has done location, unit and special photography for *Young Guns II, My Cousin Vinny, The Public Eye, The Bodyguard* and *Rapa Nui.* His images have been used extensively in national and international ad campaigns, as well as in several books published by Newmarket Press. A native of Houston, Texas, he now makes his home in Los Angeles.

FOR FURTHER VIEWING
Stagecoach, Dir. John Ford, 1939
My Darling Clementine, Dir. John Ford, 1946
Red River, Dir. Howard Hawks, 1948
She Wore a Yellow Ribbon, Dir. John Ford, 1949
Bend of the River, Dir. Anthony Mann, 1952
High Noon, Dir. Fred Zinnemann, 1952
Shane, Dir. George Stevens, 1953 *The Man from Laramie,* Dir. Anthony Mann, 1955
The Searchers, Dir. John Ford, 1956
Gunfight at the OK Corral, Dir. John Sturges, 1957
The Magnificent Seven, Dir. John Sturges, 1960
The Man Who Shot Liberty Valance, Dir. John Ford, 1962
Lawrence of Arabia, Dir. David Lean, 1962
The Naked Spur, Dir. Anthony Mann, 1963
Silverado, Dir. Lawrence Kasdan, 1985
Dances With Wolves, Dir. Kevin Coster, 1990

NOTE OF THANKS
The authors wish to thank the following people for their hours, energy and results: Esther Margolis and Newmarket Press, particularly Keith Hollaman, a deliberate man without whose calm and cool this book may not have been possible; Deborah Daly, whose unrelenting diligence and expertise is reflected on every last page; Maria Machado, for her endless time and support.

Also Jim Wilson; Kevin Costner; Moira McLaughlin; everyone at Tig Productions and Kasdan Pictures, especially Roxanne Kasdan, Anne Ward and Hugh Ross; Spooky Stevens; Elisabeth Landon and Meg Stahl at E'lan, who provided some of the interview material herein; Michael Harkavy; Diane Sponsler; Lesley North at Authoritative Word; Lindsay Beamish.

Finally, we wish to thank all of the people that made *Wyatt Earp,* those represented in this book and also the legion that we could not include here. Thank you for allowing me to watch you work, and for giving me some insight into your skilled and talented heads.

ACKNOWLEDGMENTS
We gratefully acknowledge permission to reprint copyrighted material from the following sources. *Numbers refer to pages in this book where text excerpts or illustrations appear.*

Courtesy of the Arizona Historical Society/ Tucson: i, 69, 140.

From *The Earps Talk* © 1992, ed. Alfred E. Turner. Reprinted by permission of Creative Publishing Company: 88, 101, 123.

From *The Famous Gunfighters of the Western Frontier* © 1981 by William B. Masterson. Reprinted by permission of Weatherford: 60, 68.

From *Wyatt Earp, Frontier Marshal* © 1955 by Stuart Lake. Reprinted by permission of the author's estate: 60, 97.